FROM CHAOS TO CLARITY

HOW SOCIAL WORK SKILLS CAN CHANGE YOUR LIFE

ANGEL PROTIM DUTTA

Contents

Foreword

॥ श्री गणेशाय नमः ॥

वक्रतुण्ड महाकाय सूर्यकोटि समप्रभः
निर्विघ्नं कुरु मे देव सर्वकार्येषु सर्वदा

Author's Note

Writing this book has always been a dream of mine. The idea of putting thoughts, experiences, and insights into words that could reach and inspire people is something I've always dreamt of. This book, ***"From Chaos to Clarity: How Social Work Skills Can Change Your Life,"*** is the fulfilment of that dream. I hope this book conveys the immense worth of social work as a profession and as a set of values that guide our daily actions, encouraging us to approach life with compassion and meaning.

One big reason I wanted to write the book was to address a long-standing misconception about social work. For many, the term brings to mind unpaid service—acts of charity or simply "helping society." While helping others is indeed central to social work, it is much more than that. Social work is a profession that requires knowledge, training, and specialized skills.

Like any other profession, social workers are dedicated professionals who receive compensation for their work. They are valuable for their ability to help others and their expertise in solving society's most difficult problems. This book is here to shed light on the real essence of social work and demonstrate how its skills and principles hold value far beyond the professional sphere.

We live in a society where social divides are growing with each passing day. Political arguments, cultural clashes, economic gaps, and racial tensions seem to dominate our lives. It feels harder than ever to connect with others or to find common ground. That's where this book, "From Chaos to Clarity: How Social Work Skills Can Change Your Life," comes in. It shows how the key skills of social work can help us in our daily lives.

These skills, traditionally considered a part of a profession, can also be used to create better relationships, understand others, and make communities stronger.

Most people consider social work to be a professional activity. But its skills can have a huge impact when applied in daily life. This book looks at how anyone can use these tools to promote understanding, build empathy, and create connections.

In the following chapters, we are going to closely examine skills such as active listening, empathy, communication, conflict resolution, etc. These are not just buzzwords but practical tools that can change how we relate to those around us. Each chapter will explain these skills clearly, use real-life examples, and offer exercises you can apply in your own life.

The idea of this book is to show how these skills can help us not only understand ourselves and others but also handle life's challenges with confidence. By the end of this book, you'll have the tools to strengthen relationships, navigate conflicts gracefully, and contribute to a kinder, more connected world.

This is not just a book but rather a call to action. It invites everyone who would want their world, and people within it, to become slightly better, one step at a time.

This book is for everyone else, too: whether you are a parent, a couple, or the social worker seeking to develop skills more profoundly; the student who wishes to understand the field better; the professional wanting to build strength in the community; or the person who just wishes to do better at relating and communicating with others.

I hope, no matter your background, you find inspiration and usable tools here that make a difference in your life.

As you read this book, I invite you to see social work not just as a profession but as a way of thinking and being. Let its skills and principles guide you toward a life of greater empathy, connection, and understanding.

Together, let's explore how these skills can transform not only our personal lives but also the communities we live in. Let's embark on this journey together and see how we, as humans, can evoke the potential for building a more compassionate and inclusive world.

Before going deep into pages to come, I would like to take a moment to dedicate this book to my family, mentors, and teachers who have been with me every step of the way throughout my life. Your support and encouragement have been the foundation on which I've built this journey. Without you, this dream would have remained just that—a dream!

CHAPTER ONE

FROM CHAOS TO CLARITY: SETTING THE STAGE

The first step towards making a difference is understanding why it matters

Imagine this: in a world full of hashtags, news, and constant notifications, have you ever felt like a lone sailor in the middle of a vast sea looking for a guiding light? Have you ever scrolled through endless posts and wanted real connections in all the noise? Or maybe, while dealing with your challenges, you've wondered if there's a way to navigate life's complexities?

In an age where technology both connects and isolates us at the same time, and social norms keep changing, it becomes a breeze to feel lost. People and communities face a lot of struggles, such as personal struggles, job setbacks, and family issues; finding solutions to such issues is more important than ever.

But how do we tackle these challenges? How do we learn the skills we need to thrive despite difficulties?

If any of this sounds familiar, welcome! Welcome to a journey of learning and discovery.

This book is here to answer these tough questions by using the skills and principles of social work. Whether you're a working professional, a student, a couple, or just tired of the daily grind, this book offers practical advice to help you live a more fulfilling life.

But this is not just another self-help book or a dry academic read. No, this is an invitation to look at our lives and communities differently—to see them through the lens of social work.

It's a call to action for anyone who dreams of a better, more connected world.

The core idea of this book is to use social work skills—normally used by professionals—for personal growth. It might seem a bit unconventional at first, but it actually makes a lot of sense.

The skills, principles, and ethics of social work aren't just for professionals; they are tools anyone can use to improve their life and their relationships.

WHAT IS SOCIAL WORK?

In order to understand how social work skills can help us, it is important to first know what social work is.

At its heart, social work is a profession committed to creating positive change in society. It is based on the principles of social justice and human rights. Social work aims to break down barriers, promote equality, and advocate for the welfare of all.

Social workers understand that human relationships and social systems are deeply interlinked. They strive to tackle issues like poverty, inequality, and resource scarcity by creating environments that foster healthy relationships and empower marginalized people.

Social work involves various areas, including child welfare, healthcare, education, and community development. No matter where they work, they all share a commitment towards advocacy, empowerment, and justice. They are always found at the forefront of creating a just world for future generations.

Friedlander (1951) defines, "Social work is a professional service, based on scientific knowledge and skill in human relations, which assists individuals, alone or in groups, to obtain social and personal satisfaction and independence.".

The Friedlander's definition is widely regarded as one of the most thorough explanations of social work.

It suggests that social work, similar to other professions, involves trained professionals using scientific knowledge and interpersonal skills to assist individuals and groups in achieving satisfaction both socially and personally.

A BRIEF HISTORY OF SOCIAL WORK

While understanding social work, it is also imperative to know something about its history.

Modern social work takes roots back to ancient times; however, during the time of the British colonial rule, and much later on, during India's independence movement, it gradually emerged as a modern social service.

Social welfare pioneers include Raja Ram Mohan Roy, Ishwar Chandra Vidyasagar, and Gauri Rani Banerjee among the many others, who dealt with the issues such as child marriage, caste discrimination, and rights for women.

The formalization of social work occurred when schools and universities started offering degrees in social work. The establishment of the Tata Institute of Social Sciences in Mumbai in 1936 marks a significant milestone in this regard. It played an important role in training social workers and advancing social research. After independence, the Indian government recognized that social welfare was a requirement and started designing programs to tackle poverty, education, healthcare, and inequality.

Through time, Indian social work has evolved into the activities of community and rural development, women empowerment, and advocacy.

Today, social workers in India operate in a variety of settings, including government agencies, NGOs, hospitals, schools, and grassroots organizations that collaborate with communities to effect positive change. In India, despite poverty and inequality, social workers are always committed to empowering people and making society more just.

CORE SKILLS OF SOCIAL WORK

Social work requires a wide range of skills for dealing with the complex situations social workers encounter. Here are some of the most important skills in social work:

1. Empathy

Empathy is a skill about actually understanding and sharing another person's feelings. It is one of the most basic skills that a social worker needs, as it makes it simple for social workers to communicate with clients at a more profound level.

Empathy enables social workers to view the world from the clients' perspectives, which is a crucial element in establishing trust and understanding their needs. For instance, when dealing with clients who are undergoing tough times, such as loss, grief, or trauma, empathy allows the social worker to provide emotional support to the client.

It also aids in the detection of non-verbal expressions and emotions that the clients cannot voice out. Empathy is not just about having a feeling for someone; it is the presence and giving of genuine care and concern.

2. Communication

Communication in social work is important. Social workers must communicate clearly and effectively with clients, colleagues, and other stakeholders. That means both verbal and non-verbal communication.

Verbal communication involves expressing ideas, providing information, and explaining complex concepts in ways that clients can understand.

Non-verbal communication, on the other hand, requires body language, facial movements, and look/eye contact, which convey important messages to other senses and portray feelings of empathy and acknowledgement in return.

Social workers need to become versatile in their use of communication styles with different clients, whether children, adults, or individuals from multicultural communities.
Ultimately, ensuring the client's voice during negotiations with service providers is essential.

3. Organization

Usually, a social worker will have to juggle several different cases at once, all with varying problems and needs.

Good organizational skills are required for tracking case notes, client appointments, and important deadlines.

Organization helps social workers prioritise tasks, manage their time well, and avoid leaving out any clients.

Organization also includes keeping accurate records, which are important for recording progress, measuring outcomes, and communicating with other professionals involved in a client's care.

Good organization enables social workers to provide consistent and reliable support, which is an important ingredient in gaining the trust of clients.

4. Critical Thinking

Critical thinking is the ability to analyse information, evaluate options, and make informed decisions. Critical thinking involves addressing the needs of clients, identifying deep-seated issues, and developing proper intervention plans among social work processes.

Social workers must gather information from several sources—including client interviews, medical records, and assessments—and use that information to make sound decisions.

It involves questioning assumptions, considering alternative viewpoints, and readily embracing new ideas. This skill is particularly important when working with complex cases that require creative problem-solving and flexibility.

By using critical thinking, social workers can develop effective strategies to address the needs of their clients and promote positive outcomes.

5. Active Listening

Active listening is more than just hearing what someone is saying; it involves fully concentrating, understanding, responding, and remembering what is being communicated.

Active listening is a core component of effective social work practice because it helps build trust and rapport with clients. When clients feel heard and understood, they are likely to open up and share important information.

Active listening also involves using techniques such as paraphrasing, summarising, and asking open-ended questions to encourage clients to express themselves.

Social workers help their clients feel free to voice what is concerning them because social workers listen in earnest, thus opening an area for comfort as clients disclose challenges and problems they face.

Understanding a client's need requires an appropriate intervention by applying such a skill.

6. Self-care

Social work can be very stressful for individuals in this field and expose them to problematic or even painful scenarios. Therefore, to be effective in their roles, the social worker must take time to prevent burnout by taking care of themselves.

Self-care refers to activities, among others, of relaxing, hobbies, exercise, and asking for help when required. It also refers to setting boundaries to avoid getting overwhelmed by the emotional demand of the job. Such a practice can help social workers to recharge the energy and focus needed to support their clients.

Self-care is no more a luxury but rather a necessity in sustaining a long and productive career in social work. Social workers who take good care of themselves are more likely to practice excellence with their clients.

7. Cultural Competence

It entails understanding, respecting, and effectively working well with the individuals coming from diverse cultural backgrounds.

The work of a social worker is often comprised of a multilingual clientele coming from diverse ethnic, religious, and socio-economic backgrounds.

It is vital to understand cultural differences that may influence the experiences and needs of clients. Being open to learning about diverse cultural practices, beliefs, and values and avoiding assumptions or stereotypes is part of cultural competence.

It is also important to recognise the role that systemic oppression and discrimination have played in the lives of marginalised communities.

By being culturally competent, social workers can provide more inclusive and responsive services that respect clients' identities and experiences. This skill builds a foundation for trust among the patients and helps every client to feel valued and understood.

8. Patience

Patience is one of the most important skills in the case of a social worker. Often, success in social work is gained slowly and incrementally. Clients can take time to develop trust with the social worker, disclose their experiences, or transform themselves.

Each individual's journey is unique, and the social worker should be patient enough with each of them. For those encountering trauma or who have difficulties and resist change, patience is very important.

Social workers need to offer consistent support, even if change appears minute, and mark little victories in the process. Patience also means that one needs to manage his or her expectations and that change takes time.

In being patient, social workers establish an environment that makes the clients feel motivated to move forward in the right direction of change.

9. Professional Commitment

Social work is a profession that demands commitment to lifelong learning and ethical practice. Social workers must be updated on new research, theories, and best practices to provide the most effective support to their clients.

Professional commitment involves attending workshops, pursuing further education, and staying current with changes in policies and laws that affect social work practice. Ethical practice is also a core component of professional commitment.

Social workers must adhere to a code of ethics, one that prioritises the welfare of the client, respects his autonomy, and maintains confidentiality.

In committing themselves to professional growth and ethical practice, social workers ensure they deliver the best possible service for those they are assisting.

10. Advocacy

Advocacy means standing up on behalf of clients to ensure their rights are protected and they receive the resources and services.

Social workers frequently interact with the disadvantaged and marginalised groups, and thus advocacy is used for improvement of the changes that stop the client in the fulfilment of the aims.

Advocacy may vary from helping clients to navigate complex systems to campaigning for changes in policy that promote social justice.

Social workers need to communicate effectively with policymakers, service providers, and other stakeholders to ensure that the needs of their clients are met.

Advocacy also empowers the client to speak up for themselves and gives them the tools and knowledge that they need to advocate for their own rights.

Social workers, therefore, can play a significant role in shaping a more just and equitable society by being strong advocates.

These skills, along with deep empathy and commitment to social justice, help social workers make meaningful differences in people's and communities' lives.

HOW SOCIAL WORK SKILLS CAN CHANGE YOUR LIFE

In this fast-paced, connected world, the social work skills are not just for professionals but rather are incredibly useful in everyday life as well. They help people cope with problems, form stronger relationships, and develop themselves.

Empathy, for example, allows us to connect more deeply with family, friends, and even strangers. Understanding others' feelings creates an environment where people feel valued and heard.

Active listening—listening without judging or interrupting—is also key to building good relationships. Whether it is helping a friend, handling a conflict, or even just having a casual conversation, active listening helps us connect with others.

Communication skills, both verbal and non-verbal, help us express ourselves clearly and understand others better. Whether we're negotiating, expressing gratitude, or advocating for a cause, good communication is essential for building strong relationships and achieving positive outcomes.

Social work skills are also important for self-care and resilience. Life can be overwhelming, and taking care of our mental and physical well-being helps us stay balanced. Practicing resilience, i.e., bouncing back from setbacks, helps us handle life's challenges with courage and optimism. Self-care, resilience, empathy, and active listening are all the tools that can help us live more fulfilling lives.

However, here I also would like to say that we will not go through all the skills of social work; rather, we will discuss the important ones—those that are easier to apply and most relevant to our everyday lives.

By applying these skills in our daily lives, we can grow as individuals and build a more connected and compassionate world. As you read through these pages ahead, you can better apply these skills so you're able to negotiate through difficulties in life using both strength and compassion. Let us build a better and more inclusive future for each one of us and in our community.

This book is your guide to applying social work skills in your life. Each chapter will break down a key skill, showing you how to use it in real-world situations. Through stories, examples, and exercises, you'll learn to navigate life's complexities with clarity and compassion.

The journey ahead is both personal and collective. It challenges you to grow as an individual while recognising your role in the larger community. By the end of this book, you'll have the tools to strengthen relationships, overcome challenges, and contribute to a kinder, more connected world.

Let's embark on this journey together. The first step is understanding why it matters. Let's begin.

15

EMPATHY: BEING IN THEIR SHOES

Seeing the world through their eyes, feeling the world through their hearts.

The year was 2015. My world felt like it had been turned upside down. I had just lost my dad, and the raw pain of grief threatened to consume me. During that difficult time, the unwavering support of my closest friends was a lifeline. They did not just mouth empty platitudes; they listened patiently, shared experiences of loss with me, and provided a safe space for my emotions to come out. It's such a strong reminder that empathy, being able to truly understand and share feelings, can indeed be that powerful transformer.

What made it all the more intriguing for me is what precisely this concept of empathy is and how it can be applied for positive connection to be built in everyday lives. Upon joining the Bachelor of Social Work (BSW) program at Assam Kaziranga University, Jorhat, in 2016, an introduction to the skills of social work further deepened this concept.

Before we delve deeper into this concept, allow me to ask you a question. Have you ever walked away from a conversation feeling frustrated or misunderstood? Perhaps you felt like the other person wasn't truly listening, or maybe you struggled to connect with their perspective?

In this fast-paced world, getting swept up in our own worlds often blinds us to the emotional worlds that surround us.

Here, in a nutshell, comes the role of empathy—it's a very important and powerful tool that helps in transforming our daily intercourse by making it stronger and even meaningful.

So, what is empathy? Why do we need empathy? Empathy is more than just understanding someone's feelings; it's about truly stepping into their shoes and experiencing their emotions as if they were your own.

In the context of social work, empathy is a vital skill that allows professionals to connect with individuals on a deeper level, understand their struggles, and provide meaningful support.

In general, empathy can be seen as a basis to form effective relationships between the social worker and the clients. With empathetic engagement, social workers develop rapport and trust with individuals and communities facing varied challenges. They understand and validate clients' experiences without judgement, making them feel safe and heard.

Empathy allows social workers to tailor interventions and support services for the unique needs of every client, thus fostering self-empowerment and resilience.

Furthermore, empathy makes a social worker an advocate of social justice and equality for everyone, raising the marginalized voices and challenging the system at play.

A culturally diverse empathetic social worker, adhering to the principles of cultural competence and diversity, dignifies the identity and worth of their clients while calling for inclusiveness and respect.

Through collaborative problem-solving and client-centred approaches, social workers empower clients to navigate challenges, set goals, and achieve positive outcomes.

Thus, the social work practice is built around empathy, which is a guide for the practitioners to enhance human dignity, social justice, and holistic well-being.

For instance, let's say you are a social worker seeing a client. You could easily judge them and impose your will instead of considering that addiction is a complex issue with hidden causes. But while you listen judgement-free, while you help them by accepting their struggles and showing support without stigma, that person feels safe to open up and perhaps find their way through recovery.

Empathy is not restricted to professional contexts. It applies to every other field in life. Sometimes, it could be relating to a friend going through a rough time or your family member experiencing tough challenges. In fact, some people even take up cause-related issues.

Through this, one gets the power to reach out and bring about change in someone's life positively.

As I always believe, the shortest distance between two people is empathy. It will connect you with people and help create better relationships.

The very basic definition of empathy would be the ability to understand and share the feelings of another person. It is pretty much about the F-word: feelings. Empathy is connecting with another person's emotions.

As Mary T. Lathrap, an American author, once said, you should "walk a mile in another man's shoes" if you want to understand him or his issues.

This timeless advice invites us to imagine the circumstances and challenges that someone else might be facing, enabling us to emphasize with and grasp what they are experiencing.

EMPATHY IS IMPORTANT TO ALL THE PARTS AND DIMENSIONS OF OUR LIVES

Cultivating empathy in our interactions and relationships is not only beneficial on an individual level but also contributes to the greater good of society.

When we empathize with others, we create deeper connections and foster a sense of understanding and compassion. Here's a closer look at how empathy impacts various aspects of our everyday lives:

- **Personal Relationships:** Personal relationships help people connect with their partners, relatives, and friends, creating bonding and mutual support.
  For example, when a friend is in the midst of a rough spell, empathetic listening and understanding can comfort and even encourage that friend to stand up for himself.
- **Workplace Dynamics:** In workplaces, empathy is used as a means of creating teamwork in the workplace, resolving conflicts among colleagues, and offering colleagues support.
  For example, a manager who empathizes with their team members' challenges and concerns can provide

appropriate support and resources, leading to increased morale and productivity.

Similarly, imagine a scenario where a colleague is struggling with a heavy workload and feeling overwhelmed. Instead of dismissing their concerns or offering quick solutions, you take the time to listen attentively to their challenges and acknowledge their feelings. You are validating their experiences by sympathizing with them and, as a result, providing genuine support. This will strengthen your bond, making the work environment a more supportive one.

- **Parenting:** Empathy in parenting is important for giving parents an understanding of children's emotions and perspectives. Being able to empathize with their children's experiences makes parenting nurturing and guides the creation of a supportive environment for the emotional growth and development of children.

- **Health Care Settings:** Through empathies, health care practitioners rely on the provision of quality, compassionate health care services to patients. Such quality care is enhanced if the doctors, nurses, and other health care givers empathize with fears, concerns, and experiences.

- **Community Engagement:** Empathy is very important in building strong and resilient communities. When community members empathize with each other's struggles and challenges, they come together to support and uplift one another.

For instance, neighbours helping each other during natural disasters or community members volunteering at local charities demonstrate the power of empathy in strengthening communities.

- **Conflict Resolution:** Empathy is essential for resolving conflicts peacefully and constructively. When individuals in conflict empathize with each other's perspectives and emotions, they can find common ground and work towards mutually beneficial solutions.

In a nutshell, by embracing empathy in our interactions and relationships, we enrich our lives and contribute to building a more compassionate and understanding world.

The next time you encounter someone in need of support, remember the profound impact that empathy can have and strive to extend a listening ear or a comforting shoulder, knowing that your empathy can truly make a difference.

KEEPING EMPATHY IN EVERYDAY LIFE

Now the question arises: how do we practice empathy? "How do I learn to empathize in the first place? How do I put myself in somebody else's shoes?"

Practicing empathy is a process that requires inner reflection and external actions. It is a process, not a destination, but one that takes patience, self-awareness, and a commitment to understanding and connecting with others on a deeper level.

Here are some ways I have experienced empathy as I process and grieve my father's recent passing.

1. Recalling Similar Experiences

Recalling similar experiences, whether real or through fiction, helps us practice empathy by allowing us to connect with a friend's feelings on a deeper level.

For example, imagine a scenario where your friend has lost a job. If you've never experienced losing a job, then you might think about a movie like The Pursuit of Happiness, where Will Smith's character faces the emotional toll of job loss and homelessness.

While the specifics may differ, seeing these struggles on screen can help you understand the unpredictable nature of grief or hardship.

In the same way, if you've experienced loss yourself, you can relate to the waves of emotion that come with triggers like old photographs or memories.

Drawing from these shared understandings, whether from our own lives or from a fictional portrayal, enables us to offer genuine support.

We can connect, offer comfort, and show that we truly recognize and relate to what the other person is going through, providing them with compassion and solidarity during a difficult time.

2. Be an Empathetic Listener:

This is basically the key to understanding the perspective. Pay close attention to what's being said, both verbal and non-verbal cues. Try not to interrupt or give unsolicited advice.

3. Ask Open-Ended Questions:

Show a genuine interest in their experiences by extending beyond yes or no answers. This will encourage them to give you more and better knowledge of their feelings.

For instance, sometimes you have to notice if someone's acting a little different, either positive or negative. And you can ask them, "Hey, are you okay?" or, "How are you feeling?" If somebody is happy, you can ask, "Oh, you're in a good mood. What's going on?"

Asking questions creates an open opportunity for them to say more without any pressure. Then, imagine what it must be like, whether they're in a good mood or they're having negative emotions. Come alongside them either way, to the extent that you can, and show them that you're there for them. Share their moments of difficulty or celebrate their moments of joy.

4. Consider different perspective

Try to see things from another's perspective. What can cause the person to feel that way? What experiences have they gone through that make them have this view?

5. Step out of Your Comfort Zone

Challenge your own biases and assumptions. Read books or watch documentaries about different cultures and experiences.

6. Engage with Fiction

Stories help you develop empathy. You explore emotions and situations you may not experience personally by reading about fictional characters.

7. Practice Vulnerability

Share your feelings with other people, and you shall connect more deeply with each other. Let people know you understand their struggles since you have faced challenges yourself.

8. Help Others

Whenever you see someone in need, offer your help. You can volunteer your time or simply lend a helping hand to show empathy in action.

Remember that empathy is a skill that takes time and practice to develop. With these tips, you can become more attuned to the emotions and experiences of others, which means you will be able to connect with people better and on a deeper level.

BOUNDARIES: WHY HAVING BOUNDARIES IS SOIMPORTANT?

Now, let us talk about how far we can take empathy. Is being too empathetic bad? There must always be a setting of the limits in empathy, as far as one may wish to consider the after effect of being too empathetic.

Empathy is surely significant, as it lets a person connect with others, be in their shoes, and perhaps offer support. But being too empathetic crosses boundaries between empathizing and over-emotionalization.

For example, think of a social worker who has a huge empathetic sense towards their clients in terms of traumatic experiences. His empathy drives him to the best care and support. However, he fails to set boundaries with his clients, and soon he might be emotionally drained and unable to help others as effectively in the long run.

Here's where emotional boundaries come into play. Emotional boundaries involve understanding one's own emotional resiliency and when one needs to limit one's own absorption of and engagement with others' emotions and experiences. Therapists describe this phenomenon as hyper-empathy in those people who over-empathize.

You might end up like a sponge, drinking in the sufferings and afflictions of the world and people around you, which would also include that which is done online. If you get into that bad of a mood and you know that it came from an experience, event, or what someone had to face, is this really something that you're supposed to be carrying?

Such a situation calls for the recognition of the necessity to set emotional boundaries.

Sometimes, this means taking a step back from absorbing other people's emotions. Constantly carrying the weight of others' pain can drain you, so it's important to give yourself space to recharge. It doesn't mean you care any less, but you need to protect your own emotional health.

Another way to do this is by limiting exposure to disturbing content. News and social media can be overwhelming, and constantly consuming distressing information can leave you feeling emotionally exhausted. By limiting this, you create space for your own emotions.

Lastly, seeking support from friends or colleagues is crucial. Offering empathy can take a toll, so talking to someone you trust helps you process your own feelings.

By doing so, individuals can achieve a balance between empathy toward others and self-compassion. It allows them to continue offering support and care without losing their mental and emotional well-being.

In essence, setting boundaries in empathy is practicing self-care so that we can continue empathizing and supporting others effectively while prioritizing our own well-being. Sometimes, unplugging and giving ourselves space to recharge is the best way to maintain that balance.

KEY TAKEAWAYS

- Empathy is about truly stepping into someone else's shoes and experiencing their emotions.
- In social work, empathy helps professionals connect with individuals, understand their struggles, and provide meaningful support.
- Empathy is crucial in personal relationships, workplaces, healthcare, parenting, community engagement, conflict resolution so on.
- Cultivating empathy involves recalling similar experiences, being an empathetic listener, asking open-ended questions, considering different perspectives, and practicing vulnerability.
- Setting emotional boundaries is essential to prevent burnout and ensure that empathy remains sustainable and effective.
- Taking time off from other people's emotions, restricting exposure to disturbing content, or seeking support from colleagues and friends could aid in setting boundaries.

COMMUNICATION: TALK, LISTEN, AND BOND

Every word, gesture, and silence carries the power to connect

We are social beings, wired to connect. Communication—the connection we build between ourselves and those around us—is the foundation of our existence. From the gentle murmur of a lullaby to the passionate exchange of ideas, communication shapes our experiences and interactions in every single activity we undertake.

In social work, communication is not just a transaction but becomes the basis for building trust, understanding people's needs, and empowering positive change. This chapter explores the fundamental role of communication in everyday life and social work, providing you with essential skills to do so.

WHAT IS COMMUNICATION?

Communication, at its core, is the process of exchanging information, thoughts ideas, or feelings between individuals or groups. On paper, it seems pretty simple, right? But in reality, it's not.

It is a multidimensional dynamic exchange that doesn't just involve the words but also how one uses them, how one listens, and how one responds. It can be verbal, written, gestural, facial, and even silent.

Communication is more than just talking; it's an intricate dance between speakers and listeners, where meaning is shaped by words, body language, tone of voice, and context. The way we convey a message can drastically alter its meaning.

For example, a simple "I'm fine" can mean a host of different things, such as genuine reassurance to hidden frustration, depending on tone, inflection, and facial expression. The real magic of communication is not just in the words spoken but also in the unspoken signs.

Verbal communication is the most direct way we convey thoughts and emotions. This involves spoken language. Still, even the clearest of words can carry different meanings based on how they are spoken. Tone, rhythm, and emphasis all contribute to the interpretation of the message. Take the difference between saying "I'm fine" in a cheerful voice versus a dismissive tone. Same words, but drastically different meanings.

Non-verbal communication comprises body language, facial expressions such as gestures, eye contact, etc. Often, non-verbal cues say more than words ever could. A warm smile can indicate friendliness, while crossed arms may imply defensiveness. We need to identify these signals in others and ourselves, as they can either complement, contradict, or even override verbal messages.

The art of understanding another person lies in deciphering the interplay between verbal and non-verbal communication.

We need to listen with our ears, observe with our eyes, interpret with empathy, and become like a detective piecing together those clues to really understand the meaning of a message.

COMMUNICATION: A DYNAMIC EXCHANGE

Communication is not a one-way process, but it is a dynamic exchange between the sender and the receiver. The effectiveness of a message lies not only in how it is delivered but also in how it is received.

Cultural backgrounds, personal experiences, and even individual perceptions of messages have made many misunderstandings possible in this world.

For example, if a colleague is unusually quiet or appears to pull away one wonders what it might mean—disinterest, exhaustion, or deep thought.

The responsibility lies with us to ask clarifying questions or provide additional context in order not to make assumptions and to ensure understanding.

Effective communication requires:

- Attentive listening, listening beyond the words.
- Being aware of one's own body language and tone is crucial.
- Understanding the emotions and perspective behind the words is crucial.

These skills guide us through the minefield of human connection.

ROLE OF COMMUNICATION IN SOCIAL WORK

In social work, communication is not a skill but a lifeline: it helps build trust, understand your client and their needs, and protect their rights.

Miscommunication may mean missing this opportunity. Clear, empathetic, and effective communication can be a lifesaver.

Key Functions of Communication in Social Work:

- Developing Trust and Rapport: Clients are likely to open up when they feel listened to and respected. Trust develops when social workers engage with clients as real people.
- Understanding the Client's World: Active listening helps social workers understand something unique about every individual's experiences and needs.
- Collaborative Problem-Solving: Effective communication enables both parties to work together to identify suitable solutions.
- Rights Advocacy: Social workers utilise persuasive communication to represent the needs of their clients with institutions and policymakers.

For instance, take a social worker who is working with a single mother who is struggling with childcare. By actively listening to her concerns, the social worker would understand the specific challenges facing the mother, empathize with her situation, and then advocate for support tailored to local agencies.

Effective communication turns this interaction into an empowering experience for the client.

COMMUNICATION IN DAILY LIFE

Communication in social work plays a very crucial role but is not limited to it. Communication helps us in our daily life: to build our relationships, solve conflicts, and work together practically and professionally.

Importance of Communication in Daily Life:

- **Building Relationships:** Mindful listening and responsive interaction helps intensify relationships among family and friends.
- **Resolving Conflicts:** Clear and respectful discourse helps reduce tensions and lead toward a consensus.
- **Workplace Collaboration:** Clear expression of thoughts and active listening to others enhances teamwork and productivity.
- **Engaging Communities:** Open communication fosters trust and inspires collective action in communities.

Here are some examples of how effective communication can improve our daily lives:

- **Family Circle:** Among family members, open communication strengthens relationships. A parent who pays attention to their child's problems at school shows concern and builds trust. Such an attitude creates a 'safe space' for honest discussions.

- **Workplace Collaboration:** In a workplace setting, assertive communication allows for great teamwork. An employee who comes forward with ideas in a meeting and listens to others creates an environment that makes everybody feel valued, therefore enhancing better decision-making.
- **Community Engagement:** In the community setup, clear and transparent communication helps build trust. A community leader explaining the nitty-gritty of the neighbourhoods project and offering room for comments ensures that all residents hear themselves and are, therefore, included.

BUILDING COMMUNICATION SKILLS

Effective communication in social work and everyday life takes practice and effort and increases significantly with self-awareness. Here are some practical ways to enhance your communication skills:

1. Active listening

Active listening means being completely present. Active listening involves not only hearing the words spoken, but also ensuring that one understands their meaning. Observe both the words spoken by the speaker and their body language. Do not think about how you are going to respond while they are talking; listen carefully to what they say. Use verbal cues, such as nodding, "saying I understand," or summarizing and paraphrasing what the person said to show you comprehend them.

2. Asking Open-Ended Questions

Encourage the person to make responses that go beyond a yes or no.

For instance, how did that affect your emotional state? Can you elaborate on that? This enhances the flow of the conversation and enables a deeper understanding of his feelings. This encourages the speaker to delve deeper into his thoughts, thereby providing a platform for increased interaction.

3. Be Mindful of Non-Verbal Communication

Your body language, facial expressions, and tone of voice significantly influence how others perceive your message. Maintain appropriate eye contact to show engagement, but don't overdo it.

Be mindful of your facial expressions, such as smiling when it's fitting and showing concern when discussing something serious. Your posture also matters. Leaning slightly forward shows interest, while crossing your arms can signal defensiveness.

4. Use "I" Statements

When you are talking about your feelings, use "I" statements so that you do not sound accusatory. Instead of saying, "You never listen to me," say, "I feel unheard when I try to share my thoughts." This way, you minimize defensiveness and encourage more constructive communication.

"I" statements help convey your feelings without placing blame, making it easier for others to understand your perspective.

5. Adapt to Your Audience

An effective communicator adapts his language, tone, and approach according to the audience he is talking to. You will speak to a close friend differently than you will speak to a client or a colleague.

Be sensitive to the background, experience, and emotional state of the other person. It makes sure that the message will be received well and understood.

6. Practice Empathy

Empathy is the heart of effective communication. It's about putting yourself in the other person's shoes and understanding their emotions.

Show genuine interest in what they're saying, and validate their feelings. Phrases like, "That sounds really tough," or "I can understand why you'd feel that way," help convey empathy.

Empathy fosters a deeper connection and shows the other person that you truly care.

7. Manage Emotional Reactions

Emotions can greatly affect communication. If you are angry or frustrated, take a moment. Breathe and collect your thoughts before responding.

Impulsive reactions usually lead to misunderstandings or hurt feelings.

Try to calm yourself down with deep breathing or counting to ten. Composure tends to keep the conversation more positive and productive.

8. Be Concise and Clear

Avoid over-explaining or using jargon that might confuse your listener. Aim to convey your message simply and directly.

When explaining a complex concept, break it down into simpler parts and check in with the listener to ensure they understand. Clarity is especially crucial in situations where misunderstandings could have serious consequences.

9. Reflect and Practice

Take a few minutes after a conversation to reflect on how it went. Ask yourself, "What went well?" and "What could I have done better?" This reflection will identify areas of improvement.

The best way to improve is through practice, which can be accomplished by role-playing difficult conversations with a friend or colleague.

10. Give and Take Feedback

Constructive feedback is necessary for improving communication skills. Let people know how you think they communicate with you, and be open to changing your communication style.

Similarly, give feedback to others in a respectful manner. When giving feedback, focus on the specific behaviours and avoid personalizing.

For instance, say, "I observed that while you were speaking, you hardly maintained eye contact," rather than saying, "You are not a good communicator."

Communication is the basis of all human interactions, whether it's in our personal relationships, professional environments, or in social work. It is the tool that helps us build trust, resolve conflicts, and collaborate effectively.

In social work, communication is particularly crucial because it can be the difference between understanding and misunderstanding, between helping someone and missing an opportunity to make a positive impact.

With effective communication, which we enhance by being active listeners, empathetic towards the audience, mindful, and able to change our message according to the audience, we enhance our ability to connect with people as well as empower ourselves in making meaningful and long-lasting changes.

Communication is not only what is spoken but also action, body language, and the empathy that comes along with the words. It is the bridge that connects us, and mastering it is important for a more compassionate and connected world.

IN A NUTSHELL

- **Communication is a Dynamic Exchange:** Effective communication is not only about sending a message but also about how it is received. Always be attentive to the listener's reactions and be prepared to clarify or adjust your approach.
- **Empathy is the Key:** Empathy is the foundation when relating to others and creating a proper, meaningful connection. Practice being the other person and respond with compassion.
- **Nonverbal Signals Matter:** Communication is a combination of words, body language, tone, and face to convey and interpret meanings.
- **Active Listening Builds Trust:** The ability to truly listen to others builds trust and understanding. Show you are paying attention by responding thoughtfully and summarizing what has been said.
- **Adjust Your Communication Style:** Every person is different, and effective communication is adjusting your approach based on the needs of your audience.

CHAPTER FOUR

ACTIVE LISTENING: THE HEART OF CONNECTION

To hear what's unsaid is the essence of active listening

In this chapter, we'll be discussing another important skill in social work, i.e., active listening. Before we delve deeper, may I ask you a question? Have you ever experienced trying to share something important with friends, colleagues, or family members, only to have them start talking about themselves instead of truly listening to you? Or perhaps someone abruptly interrupted you mid-conversation? How did that make you feel? Probably pretty disheartened, right? It can feel as though someone is undervaluing your thoughts and feelings, or as though they're overshadowing you in a conversation.

Drawing from my personal experiences, I often observe that during family meetups or office meetings, we tend to interrupt others in between conversations, rather than listening to what they have to say. While this may temporarily give us the upper hand, it's important to consider the perspective of the person on the other side of the corner. Empathy! Right? Have you ever wondered why courts have the ability to provide better judgements? It is because they listen to both sides!

If you find yourself saying yes to all these questions, then let me tell you, my friend, you are not alone. We've all been there. The damage caused by these types of behaviour is immense. It could result in never sharing anything with the person again, or it could lead to misunderstandings or conflicts between the two, as neither party truly listens to the other. At the very least, it could lead to a loss of respect for the other person.

Because of this, active listening is a highly valued skill in social work that a social worker must master in order to become a seasoned social worker.

Now, you might be wondering, "What is active listening and how is it different from the listening we do in general?"

Active listening is a skill that involves not only paying attention to what the speaker is saying but also to their intentions and emotions behind it. It involves asking the right questions for understanding the complete situation.

In the context of social work, active listening refers to listening to the client attentively with empathy, trying to understand the situation and the problem, and asking the right questions by using techniques like summarising or paraphrasing so that the social worker can understand the full situation and can provide the best possible solution to the client's problems.

It aids in building trust and fostering a positive environment, which in turn allows the client to feel comfortable and share more, ultimately fostering a positive professional relationship. This will assist in providing a customized solution to the client.

Let us understand how this active listening works with an example. Imagine that a client suffering from depression approached a social worker in search of assistance.

The client expressed, "I feel helpless; nobody in my family understands me." My family is constantly arguing over trivial matters, which is negatively impacting all facets of life. I feel sad.".

The social worker: Your family's conflict appears to be causing you a great deal of distress. I understand that the constant fighting and tension must be extremely draining for you.

Can you tell me more about the situation? What is the reason for the family conflict, and how is it impacting you?

In this example, the social workers, rather than placing blame on the family or isolating the client, demonstrated empathy and summarised the situation effectively. The social worker then asked the appropriate questions to identify the reasons and how the situation is affecting the client. This fostered a continuous flow of conversation. The social worker was only able to identify the issue because he actively listened to what the client was sharing.

Similarly, like in social work, active listening can be a powerful tool in our day-to-day life. Active listening can solve 90% of our problems, according to research. The majority of our daily problems, regardless of their size, stem from poor listening skills.

Example: You're running late for work, and your mother has asked you to bring some groceries. However, in your haste, you didn't pay attention and instead went to the office. When you returned home, your mother inquired about the groceries you had neglected to bring. Happened? Perhaps your boss instructed you to draft the meeting minutes. But due to a lot of discussions going on, you forgot the key points. Happened?

The client requested specific details to be included in the report you will be sending them in a week. You shared the reports but forgot to include the specific points. Happened? You may argue that this did not occur due to poor listening; there are other factors at play. Undoubtedly, poor listening is one of those reasons.

There are many benefits of using active listening in our daily life. These are –

- **Reduces chances of misunderstanding:** Using active listening can help in reducing chances of misunderstanding a person or concept by clarifying information, confirming perspective, and understanding perspectives.
  For example, students actively listen to the teacher and ask questions to clarify doubts when needed.
- **Strengthen or build relationships:** Active listening, by demonstrating interest, empathy, and respect in what the other person is saying, aids in both strengthening existing relationships and fostering the development of new ones.
  Whether it's family, professional, or relationships with a spouse, girlfriend, or boyfriend, active listening strengthens these relationships and creates a positive atmosphere for sharing information.
  Similarly, meeting a stranger and listening to their side of the story can also help build new relationships. This phenomenon is more evident in social media platforms like Facebook, Instagram, WhatsApp, and so on.
  Another example could be our relationships with the singers. By listening to their songs, we fall in love with

their voice, which creates a bond with them. Whether we have met them in person or not, we have a strong relationship with them. I vividly recall being shocked and devastated when my favourite singer, Krishnakumar Kunnath, also known as "KK," passed away in 2022. Thus, active listening can have a profound impact on one's life.

- **Conflict resolution:** While active listening is key to reducing misunderstandings, it is also key to resolving conflicts. Employing active listening in everyday life, we can solve conflicts and avoid them.

  As an example, couples who practice active listening and open communication can work on finding common ground.

  Similar to this, if we can listen to each other and try to find a common ground, we can avoid or resolve conflicts in the workplace.

- **Increased Trust:** Active listening builds trust and rapport by demonstrating sincerity, reliability, and attentiveness.

  An example could be a therapist or a doctor, actively listening to us, creating a safe and trusting environment for sharing our experiences.

- **Improved leadership skills:** To be a leader, one has to have the skill of active listening. It improves our leadership skills by making us trustworthy and loyal.

  For example, a manager, by actively listening to his/her team, can understand the concerns related to work distribution or challenges they encounter in completing the task.

  Aids in effective decision-making: By employing active listening, one can make informed decisions by gathering all the perspectives, insights, and information.

- **Personal Growth:** Active listening promotes personal growth by encouraging us to be self-aware, open-minded, as well as empathetic.

These are some of the benefits of active listening. You may be wondering how to cultivate this skill of active listening.

TECHNIQUES FOR ACTIVE LISTENING

Listening is a skill that most of us possess, but not all of us are proficient listeners. Unlike other skills, we can cultivate or enhance active listening. While most of us possess the ability to engage in active listening, we often fail to use it effectively.

Research says that people who haven't honed their listening skills typically retain only about 50% of a conversation immediately after it occurs; within 48 hours, this figure drops to less than 25%. While it's true that active listening requires effort, it is a valuable skill to hone.

Different noises bombard us throughout the day, but not all of them demand our focused attention. Thus, it is crucial to discern when and how to employ active listening effectively.

Whether it's in the workplace, during important meetings, in educational settings, or in simple discussions with friends and family, active listening can greatly enhance the communication and understanding.

Now let us understand how to improve active listening skills.

1. Paying attention to the speaker

As mentioned earlier, active listening is not just about hearing what the speaker is saying; it's about paying attention to what he/she is saying as well as their intent and emotion behind it. Avoid distractions like talking on the phone or looking away. Without these, simply listening won't do the trick.

Example: Imagine you are in a class where the teacher is explaining a crucial math problem; just simply listening to the teacher won't make you understand the problem.

You need to pay attention, understand intent and formulas, and then only you'll be able to solve the problem. Conversely, the teacher can only facilitate your understanding if you are attentive; if you are distracted, no amount of lecture can help you understand any concept.

2. Show that you are listening

While listening, it's crucial to demonstrate our attentiveness by showing the speaker that we're paying attention.

We can do this by simply using non-verbal cues such as nodding and maintaining eye contact. By doing this, we can see the speaker's expression, whether he/she is angry, sad, or happy, ultimately allowing us to understand their emotions.

3. Limit your talking

"Limit your talk" emphasizes the importance of letting the speaker express themselves fully without interruptions or asking silly questions. By limiting our own talking, we create an environment where the speaker shares their perspectives uninterrupted.

This approach fosters a more meaningful exchange where the speaker feels heard and valued. It's not about us speaking very little or not at all; it's about actively listening to the speaker's side of the story, asking meaningful questions, and giving them the opportunity to respond fully. This genuine engagement in the conversation helps build stronger and more meaningful relationships.

4. Hold your judgements

While listening to someone else's story, it is very easy to jump to conclusions or judge the person. Imagine yourself sharing your story, and someone gives you a biased opinion. How would you feel? Bad, right? Avoiding hasty judgments is a vital component of active listening.

Let me tell you why, often, the initial conversation provides a very limited perspective; holding off our judgements helps us get a complete picture of the story.

Similarly, refraining from making judgments allows us to consider alternative perspectives, thereby avoiding biased opinions. We should always refrain from making judgments, and we can achieve this by asking questions to fill in any gaps in our understanding of the speaker's message. It will not only enhance our communication skills but also aid in making better decisions and building strong relationships.

5. Being in their shoes

While listening to/responding to the speaker, we should try to put ourselves in the speaker's shoes, meaning try to see things from the speaker's perspective. Think how you would feel if you were in that situation. This is all about developing empathy toward the speakers.

6. Ask the right questions

We've been talking about asking the right questions throughout this chapter. This involves posing thoughtful questions and allowing the speaker to provide further details. These questions should be "open-ended," meaning they go beyond "yes" or "no" answers and invite further explanations.

Imagine this: you have shared something important to you, and the listener remains blank, didn't ask any questions, or didn't even nod. How would you feel? This is where asking the right questions comes in.

Although we don't learn listening, it's one of the most crucial skills. Good listening helps us to easily connect with others and build relationships. Most of the listening we do in our daily lives is passive, meaning we listen without paying proper attention. Active listening is the complete opposite of passive listening.

It's about investing significant mental energy in understanding what the speaker is saying. Next, you should actively listen to the speaker, refrain from straying from the topic or sharing your personal experiences, formulate meaningful questions, summarize the speaker's points, and allow the speaker to speak without interruption.

Patience is the key—once they've done enough talking, they will give you the opportunity to share your side of the story as well.

In essence, active listening isn't just about hearing words. It's about understanding, connecting, and nurturing meaningful connections.

KEY HIGHLIGHTS

- Active listening is giving your full attention and tuning into words, body language, and emotions. It makes the speaker feel truly heard.
- Use cues like nodding, eye contact, and "mmhmm" to show you're engaged. It reassures the speaker that you are genuinely concerned.
- Refrain from hastily drawing conclusions. Delaying judgment allows you to fully comprehend the story before responding.
- Ask questions that are open-ended enough to encourage deeper sharing. It demonstrates genuine curiosity and ignites meaningful dialogue.
- Put yourself in the speaker's shoes to truly understand their perspective. Empathy really creates deeper connections.

CHAPTER FIVE

52

ORGANIZATION SKILLS: A ROADMAP TO SUCCESS

An ordered life is a balanced life in which clarity leads to productivity and peace of mind.

An organized life is not about clean or effective management at work but is built on systems that give direction, some structure, and a sense of purpose. Organization actually means building processes that enable the proper use of time, resources, and responsibilities; for many people, an organized life becomes balanced, clear, and able to achieve goals without any sense of overwhelm.

Organizational skills are important in both professional and personal lives. They can keep us on track with our tasks, help us prioritize them, and bring joy to the ordinary by reducing chaos. Whether a social worker manages multiple cases or a parent juggles household chores, organization is key to productivity and peace of mind.

ORGANIZTIONAL SKILLS ARE CRUCIAL FOR A SOCIAL WORKER

Organization is a skill social workers must master, among all others. A social worker manages clients' needs, coordinates with agencies, advocates for resources, and maintains records in detail. The only thing that stands between them and a forgotten client or concern is meticulous organization.

Why organizational skills remain the backbone of social work?

- **Managing High Caseloads:** Social workers manage many clients by making sure everything is in its proper place.

- **Meeting Deadlines:** Proper planning allows the social worker to meet critical deadlines in responding to crises, filing reports, or securing resources for clients.
- **Stakeholders:** One requires good organizational skills when working collaboratively with clients, agencies, and policymakers in order to ensure good communication and follow-up.
- **Diminishes stress and burnout:** A structured approach to work helps an individual manage stress and prevent burnout, thereby focusing and energizing a social worker.

For instance, consider a social worker who is assisting a family in distress. She needs to gather information about housing options, schedule therapy sessions, and complete paperwork.

A clear plan enables the smooth completion of these tasks, ensuring the family receives timely support. Without strong organizational skills, a social worker could easily overlook critical steps, leading to delays in providing help.

HOW TO DEVELOP ORGANIZATIONAL SKILLS IN DAILY LIFE

You can apply social work skills in the workplace and in general life. Acquiring organizational skills will bring smoother routines, productivity, and fulfilment to your day.

There are several approaches to creating organizational habits that are meaningful in life:

1. Manage Your Time

Time is a scarce resource, and its management is essential in life and at the workplace. Social workers have very tight schedules, leaving them with little time for themselves. The management makes sure to complete the work efficiently and without wasting time in unfavourable conditions.

Here are some practical tips on how to achieve this:

- **Use the planner:** Schedule all your activities, meetings, and downtime in a planner or calendar application, but avoid missing an important commitment. It is as simple as writing down all the tasks and events happening for the week.
  For instance, a working woman could use a planner to schedule office meetings, school activities for her children, and important family gatherings, thereby avoiding any missed events and maintaining a daily plan.
- **Set Priorities:** High-risk situations require the first accomplishment of urgent matters. Prepare a list of all tasks and decide which should receive primary attention.
  For instance, in the case of a business owner, he/she has to attend to the immediate needs of clients and legal documentation first and not routine admin matters.
- Take Breaks: Just like social workers need time off from work to not burn out, take breaks within your day to

refresh your mind. That could be a 15-minute chai (tea) break after doing something big. It keeps you energetic and alert for longer.

2. Setting Priorities

Social workers face competing demands to meet the immediate needs of their clients while working on long-term goals. A prioritised list helps them to know what really matters and to not miss the small stuff.

Practical Tips

- **The Eisenhower Matrix:** The Eisenhower Matrix is a simple tool to help you manage your time and focus on what truly matters. Start by listing all your tasks, then divide them into the four quadrants of the matrix below.

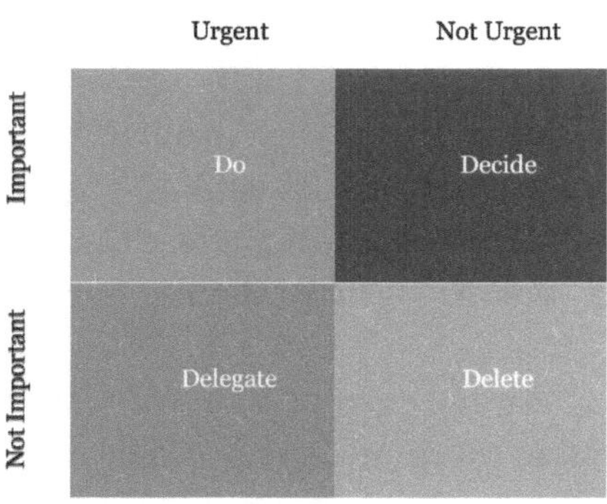

Figure 1: The Eisenhower Matrix

a) Tasks that are **urgent and important**, write them in the "Do" quadrant—these need your immediate attention, like solving a critical issue.

b) Tasks that are **important but not urgent** belong in the "Decide" quadrant. Plan these for later, such as organizing or strategizing.

c) For tasks that are **urgent but not important**, place them in the "Delegate" quadrant. Let someone else handle these to save your time.

d) Finally, tasks that are neither urgent nor important are placed in the "Delete" quadrant. Eliminate these distractions altogether. By using this matrix, you can clearly see where to focus your efforts and how to handle everything efficiently.

- **Breaking Big Goals:** Take big goals and break them into smaller, manageable tasks.

For instance, if you want to renovate your house, you may first break it down into such small tasks as choosing a contractor, budgeting, and buying materials. It makes the whole process less intimidating and ensures steady progress.

3. Clean up your physical and digital space.

A messy space creates mental clutter, which slows down and distracts from productivity. Social workers need a clean, organized workspace where they can quickly fetch client files, gather their material, and stay organized. Similarly, a neat workspace facilitates focus and effectiveness, making our daily lives easier.

How to Do It: Practical Tips

- **Organize physical spaces:** Make designated places for important things at home or work so you don't waste too much time looking for them. In a typical Indian household, you could have a specific place to put keys, bills, and other important documents. It saves much time on hectic mornings.
- **Manage Digital Resources:** Keep your desktop/laptop/ mobile clean. Back up important documents. Place emails into folders. Build folders for different types of emails, such as those from family, work, or finances. This makes accessing emails easier. For instance, you can organise your email inbox to make it easier to find a transaction receipt when managing your monthly expenses.
- **One in, one out:** If you are introducing a new thing, then you have to eliminate something to keep that space uncluttered. So if you purchase a new kurta/shirt, discard the older ones that you do not wear. This helps you maintain control and balance in your wardrobe.

4. Planning and scheduling

Planning is required for the management of such commitments, including case evaluations and home visits. Without a plan, individuals may easily overlook important tasks or deadlines, leading to undesirable consequences.

Follow these practical tips to achieve the following:

- **Weekly planning:** Set aside some time to plan for the entire week. It would take 15 to 20 minutes on a Sunday evening to plan for the following week, which could include everything from work meetings to grocery planning to family time.
- **Using Technology:** Utilise digital tools such as Trello, Notion, or even reminders on your phone to monitor your tasks, due dates, and schedules. Set Google Calendar reminders for paying bills or attending social events, among other things, to never miss anything.
- **Plan for the Unpredictable:** Account for some time to face unforeseen situations. If you are traveling to work, consider the possibility of experiencing traffic congestion during your journey. If you prepare for this, you can handle any unexpected event with ease.

5. Be Flexible

Most social workers experience a shift in client needs, policies, and even crises. Flexibility is the key to being productive. The same applies in personal life, where unexpected situations may crop up and disrupt one's plans.

Practical Tips:

- **Be Solution-Oriented:** Instead of dwelling on setbacks when plans change, concentrate on what you can do. For instance, if you're unable to attend a meeting due to traffic, offer to join virtually. This approach ensures the achievement of the objective despite any setbacks.
- **Re-Evaluate Priorities:** Change the schedule based on shifting priorities. If there is an emergency family situation, prepare to get less important work done at another time. This ensures that you address the important matters first.
- **Be resilient and believe in every situation:** Understand that difficulties are opportunities for increasing problem-solving skills. Consider the power outage at home as an opportunity to spend quality time with your family, free from electronic distractions. Helps build resilience and adaptability.

Bringing order to everyday life:

Here's how you can apply these techniques to bring some kind of order into your daily routine:

- Start your day by evaluating the goals and planning toward their fulfilment. A great morning routine can really set up a good vibe for the rest of the day. For example, spend an hour doing some yoga or meditation, followed by planning out your day.

- Make a checklist. To-do lists help one stay focused and track his progress daily or weekly. Crossing off tasks makes one feel accomplished. For example, create a grocery checklist before going to the market.
- Reflect and review. Every day, evaluate your actions and what you could have done better. Growth happens, and the ability to adapt remains intact.

For example, a person can reflect on how he has performed in getting things done at home and at work.

Good organizational skills can transform personal and professional lives. They bring clarity, reduce stress, and help you accomplish tasks and meet goals on time. By incorporating these skills, you can boost productivity and achieve a healthier work-life balance.

To be organized is to weave a life worth living, not mere task management. With the principles of prioritizing, flexibility, and even time management, you can organize your entire life with purpose and meaning. START SMALL, remain consistent, and watch how you improve every day.

ESSENTIAL INSIGHTS

- **Organization is crucial**, whether one is working in social work or managing life, both of which require structure to yield productivity and satisfaction.
- **Time Management is Crucial:** Use planners and digital calendars to keep track of your schedule. Prioritize Focus on things that are urgent and important and decompose big goals into workable tasks.
- **Declutter regularly:** Maintain a clean real and virtual world to keep your brain on track and focused.
- **Plan and be flexible:** plan one's week, utilize digital tools, and be prepared to change as circumstances change. Small steps at first will finally result in massive improvement with respect to productivity and life balance.
- **Reflect Daily:** Evaluate what worked well and where there is room for improvement to keep growing.
- **Celebrate Successes:** Recognize and celebrate organizational successes, no matter how small, for keeping them motivated.
- **Use Technology to Help Implement:** Utilise apps and digital tools to organise and otherwise assist in efforts to organise.

CHAPTER SIX

THE ART OF CRITICAL THINKING

Critical thinking is not about being right; it's about exploring perspectives, asking questions, and seeking clarity in complexity.

Critical thinking is the ability to think clearly and rationally and to reflect on the logical connection between ideas. It involves objective analysis of information, questioning of assumptions, and evaluation of evidence to make sound judgments. Critical thinking is not mere knowledge acquisition; it is how we apply knowledge in solving problems and mastering the complexities in life.

In a way, critical thinking is acting like an active learner as opposed to a passive recipient of information. This requires curiosity, skepticism, and an open mind to explore new possibilities. For social workers and people in general, it is a powerful tool enhancing the quality of decision-making processes leading to better outcomes.

SIGNIFICANCE OF CRITICAL THINKING IN SOCIAL WORK

Critical thinking is an essential skill in social work. Social workers are often faced with complex situations where they have to make decisions that impact the well-being of others.

The ability to assess situations objectively, consider multiple perspectives, and evaluate evidence is crucial for effective practice. Here are some reasons why critical thinking is vital in social work:

- **Enhanced Good Practices for Clients:** Critical thinking provides valuable understanding of the needs of social care clients and aids in the development of intervention strategies. It could design solutions that are specifically tailored to each individual's circumstances, leading to the best possible outcomes.

- **Ethical Decision-Making:** Social workers often face ethical dilemmas that involve conflicting interests. Critical thinking gives them the ability to make judgements about the possible results of various actions and choose ones that are in line with standards of ethics.
- **Effective Problem-Solving:** Social workers face various issues, from unresolved conflict between family members to mental issues. Critical thinking aids social workers in identifying the primary issue, devising various strategies to address it, and selecting the most effective approach to improve the situation.
- **Advocacy and policy influence:** Critical thinking helps social workers analyze policies and advocate for changes that benefit their clients. They can identify gaps by critically evaluating the effectiveness of the existing policies and propose improvements.

CRITICAL THINKING IN REAL LIFE

Our personal lives also greatly benefit from critical thinking. Be it the choice of accepting which job offer, deciding the credibility of news sources, or the best way to invest your savings, critical thinking helps in making informed choices.

For instance, if you were to buy a car, critical thinking would enable you to compare models, assess their features, read reviews, and even consider factors such as fuel efficiency and maintenance costs. Instead of relying on advertisements or sales pitches, you analyze the available information objectively to make the best decision based on your needs.

A practical application of critical thinking is relational handling. As soon as an argument arises, it helps the person understand why the other person acted in that way and find constructive methods to resolve the problem. Rather than letting emotions rule the moment, you think before you react for healthier relationships.

HOW TO DEVELOP CRITICAL THINKING IN DAILY LIFE

Developing critical thinking skills takes practice and intentionality. Here are some tips to help you cultivate critical thinking in your daily life:

1. Ask questions.

Curiosity forms the basis of critical thinking. When a situation, a bit of information, or a decision is brought before them, they ask thoughtful questions, such as:

- Why is it happening?
- What are its underlying causes?
- What is the evidence supporting this claim?
- Do other explanations exist?

For example, if you hear a news story, don't just accept it at face value. Dig deeper. Who is the source? What might their agenda be?

By asking these questions, you challenge assumptions and ensure that you're working with accurate and unbiased information.

2. Consider Multiple Perspectives

Critical thinking involves looking at issues from various angles. Before making a decision or forming an opinion, take a step back and consider:

- How would another person look at this issue?
- What are the advantages and disadvantages of alternative strategies?
- How will this decision impact other people?

For example, when working to resolve a workplace dispute, consider how each party sees the situation. This approach will enhance your understanding of each party's perspective and result in more equitable and balanced outcomes.

3. Be aware of and combat biases.

We all have personal biases that influence the way we think. Recognizing and challenging these biases is a hallmark of critical thinking.

- Start by identifying your own biases.
- Are there certain assumptions or beliefs you hold that could cloud your judgement?
- Be open to changing your mind when presented with new evidence.

For instance, if you think your colleague is difficult to work with, ask yourself: Is this because of one incident or a series of incidents? Am I basing it on rumours or personal preferences?

By checking these biases, you approach situations much more objectively.

4. Weigh evidence.

In the era of information, not all data is equal. Learning to develop critical thinking is the process of assessing the quality and reliability of evidence before drawing conclusions.

- Is the source credible?
- Are the data points current and relevant?
- Is there sufficient evidence to support the claim?

For instance, if one is researching a healthy diet or financial investment, it is not sufficient to base decisions on anecdotal evidence. Instead, one must look for peer-reviewed studies, expert opinions, or historical data. The core of effective decision-making relies on reliable evidence.

5. Practice decisions.

Critical thinking and decision-making go hand in hand. Make decisions by weighing various choices and considering their outcomes.

- List the advantages and disadvantages of each decision.

- Consider the immediate and long-term implications.
- Think of the ethical and practical impacts.

For instance, when choosing between two job offers, don't just focus on the salary. Think about career growth, work-life balance, and company culture. Practicing this methodical approach to decisions strengthens your critical thinking muscles.

6. Engage in discussions and debates.

Discussion with other people, especially those who hold different opinions, is one of the best ways to hone your critical thinking. This forces you to defend your ideas against their opposing views, exposes you to new perspectives, and allows you to improve your reasoning.

- Engage in discussions about topics you care about or feel passionate about.
- Listen to others' opinions without immediately reacting negatively.
- Express your opinion clearly, respectfully, and with evidence.

For instance, discussion of a social issue with friends, attending a book club or participating in professional roundtable discussions may offer some quality time to test and hone your critical thinking.

7. Reflect on Your Thinking Process

Critical thinking involves not only the evaluation of external information but also an analysis of the thought process.

Take some time to reflect on how you go about solving problems or making decisions.

Ask yourself: Have I considered all relevant factors? Have emotions or biases influenced me?

Reflect on what you might do differently the next time to enhance your thinking.

Journaling your thoughts or reflecting on past decisions can be an excellent way to practice this self-reflection.

8. Be Open-Minded

Critical thinking feeds off of flexibility. Being open to new ideas, perspectives, and ways of thinking allows you to adapt and grow.

- Avoid making hasty judgments or rigidly adhering to a particular perspective.
- Be able to concede when you're wrong, or when new evidence surfaces and alters your perspective

For instance, in a professional environment, if a colleague proposes an unconventional approach to a project, refrain from dismissing it abruptly. Examine it objectively and determine if it could potentially yield greater effectiveness.

9. Exercise critical thinking in real-life situations.

To effectively cultivate critical thinking, integrate it into your daily routines:

- **Reading News:** When reading the news, don't blindly accept headlines. Look into the sources, verify facts, and consider multiple angles.
- **Shopping Decisions:** When buying a product, compare reviews, check specifications, and consider long-term value instead of just going for the cheapest or trendiest option.
- **Problem solving at work:** break down complex problems into smaller parts, analyze root causes, and brainstorm solutions collaboratively.

More you use critical thinking daily, the more it will feel natural to you.

10. Growth Mindset:

Critical thinking is not a fixed ability; rather, it is something that improves with effort. Cultivate a mindset of learning, growth, and constructive feedback.

- Treat failures as learning experiences rather than as failures.
- Seek out new experiences that challenge your way of thinking.

For instance, taking up a new hobby, learning a foreign language, or travelling to unfamiliar places can broaden your horizons and enhance your critical thinking abilities.

Critical thinking is one of the most valuable skills because it helps us think more critically about our professional and personal lives.

In social work, it helps the practitioners make appropriate decisions, solve problems in an effective manner, and advocate for their clients. In our daily lives, it helps us make better choices, understand different perspectives, and approach challenges with a rational mindset.

Critical thinking requires practice, the desire to know, and challenging assumptions. Through questioning and considering alternative perspectives, observing biases, analyzing evidence, and having thoughtful discussions, we learn to think critically and thereby make informed decisions that lead to positive outcomes.

REFLECTIONS & LEARNINGS

- **Ask Questions:** Be curious and question everything. Asking questions helps one dig deeper and gain a better understanding of any situation.
- **Consider Multiple Perspectives:** Don't limit yourself to one viewpoint. Explore different angles to understand the full picture.
- **Reflect on Biases:** Be aware of your own biases and challenge them to ensure objective thinking.
- **Evaluate Evidence:** Always assess the quality and reliability of the information you have before forming conclusions.
- **Practice Decision-Making:** Weigh pros and cons, consider potential outcomes, and make informed decisions.
- **Engage in Discussions:** Participate in debates and discussions to challenge your thinking and understand opposing views.

With these skills and insights, you're better equipped to think critically, make informed decisions, and lead a life of purpose and clarity.

CHAPTER SEVEN

TURNING CONFLICT INTO OPPORTUNITIES

*Within each conflict is the potential for the emergence of
new understanding and growth.*

Conflict is inevitable and manifests in individuals' personal and professional lives, as well as other spheres where disagreements may arise due to individual perceptions, requirements, or perceived worth. Even though conflicts can be unpleasant and lead to numerous problems, they are not inherently evil. It can turn into an experience of growth, a place for understanding and bridges to form when managed positively. Let us discuss the art of conflict resolution, equipping you with tools and strategies to negotiate your way out of conflicts as well as turn challenges into meaningful opportunities for change.

UNDERSTANDING CONFLICT: NATURE AND DYNAMICS

Conflict, in essence, is a natural phenomenon of human interaction. It arises whenever individuals or groups perceive that their goals, interests, or values are incompatible. While a negative approach to conflict often garners attention, a constructive approach remains enduring.

In "The Resolution of Conflict: Constructive and Destructive Processes," Morton Deutsch stated that the management of conflicts determines their outcome. Poor management can lead to resentment and even division, while constructive management fosters better understanding and cooperation.

The Two-Fold Nature of Conflict:

• **Destructive Conflict:** Avoided, escalated, or handled aggressively, conflict is associated with broken relationships, poor trust, and little productivity.

• **Constructive Conflict:** If respected, empathized, and with a problem-solving intent, conflict can unearth unseen problems, strengthen relationships, and build solutions.

Anger, frustration, and fear are the most common sources of disagreement in conflict dynamics, while empathy and understanding support de-escalation. Emotional Intelligence, by Daniel Goleman, holds that control over your own emotions is the hallmark of constructive conflict resolution.

CONFLICT RESOLUTION IN SOCIAL WORK

Conflict resolution is an essential skill for social workers. Social workers have to work out conflicts with professionalism and empathy, whether mediating between family members, advocating for clients, or addressing systemic injustices.

Social Work Approaches to Conflict Resolution

• **Mediation:** Facilitating dialogue between conflicting parties to reach a mutually acceptable agreement.
• **Advocacy:** Representing clients' needs and rights in conflicts with institutions or systems.

- **Empowerment**: Helping clients develop the skills and confidence to address their conflicts constructively.

For example, a social worker working between the estranged couple who co-parent the child can apply the skills of active listening and reframing to guide the couple away from accusations of how they are wrong in parenting to solutions of how they can collectively care for their child.

CONFLICT IN DAILY LIFE

Conflict can manifest in various forms, ranging from a simple argument to a full-blown dispute. Understanding the causes of conflict in daily life can help individuals better manage their disputes.

Common causes of conflict

- **Miscommunication:** Some conflicts are due to unnecessary assumptions or misheard words.
- **Conflicting Values or Beliefs:** Disputes arise due to conflicting belief systems, especially the emotion-sensitive ones, such as politics or religion.
- **Competing Needs or Interests:** The competition for resources, time, and focus frequently leads to conflict.
- **Unclosed Past Issues:** Typically, unresolved past disagreements between parties lead to conflicts, creating a festering sore.
- **Parent-Child Dispute:** This issue can potentially lead to conflict between parents and teenagers, as the teenager often harbours hidden issues with their parents.

- **Work Conflicts:** Some workers experience pressure due to feelings of mistreatment or poor communication regarding equitable opportunities.
- **Community Conflicts:** Typically, projects or issues that impact the community, such as new development or zoning amendments, lead to differences in priorities among the residents.

CONFLICT RESOLUTION VIA SOCIAL WORK SKILLS

Effective conflict resolution addresses the underlying issues and ensures the respect and hearing of all parties. The following tips, based on social work and communication studies, guide the construction of conflict resolution:

1. Focus on interests, not positions.

Positions are demands or claims, and interests are needs and concerns. Fisher, Ury, and Patton, in their book **"Getting to Yes: Negotiating Agreement Without Giving In,"** said that shifting the emphasis from position to interest will often enable people to collaborate.

Example: When scheduling a workplace grievance, parties may talk about the needs and concerns underlying rigid demands ("I need mornings off!") rather than the former.

2. Active Listening

Actually hearing the other party is crucial for resolving conflict. This entails refraining from interrupting the speaker, interpreting their words to ensure comprehension, and acknowledging the emotion they are expressing.

Example: A spouse expressing frustration about household responsibilities might feel validated if their partner says, "It sounds like you're feeling overwhelmed because you're handling most of the chores."

3. Separate people from the problem

Personalizing the issue will inevitably lead to confrontation and escalate the situation. Turn this into a statement that focuses on how to solve the problem.

For instance, instead of saying, "You never listen to me," consider saying, "I feel unheard and bypassed when decisions are made quickly without discussion."

4. Express empathy and respect.

This means you acknowledge others' feelings and views, especially in case you don't see things their way. Respect is always a healthy atmosphere for positive communication.

5. Integration of problem-solving skills.

Strive to find win-win solutions that address all needs. This would require generating ideas and collaborating to achieve the optimal result.

CONFLICT RESOLUTION STRATEGIES

You can apply practical skills for conflict resolution in any possible setting. These are, as research has proven, really applicable in real-life settings—personal, professional, or community.

a) De-escalation skills.

- **Pause and Reflect**: This will help avoid impulsive acts.
- **Lower Your Tone**: If one keeps quiet, people would normally lower their volume to match his.
- **Reflect Emotions**: Acknowledge and validate the person's feelings without judging them. Instead of evaluating their emotions, show understanding and empathy.

This helps reduce defensiveness and creates a safe space for open communication.

b) Negotiation skills.

- **Prepare Well**: Know what your needs are and what the other party may want.
- **Seek Common Ground**: Find common ground to create momentum towards a resolution.
- **Maintain Flexibility**: Show a willingness to explore unconventional approaches to establish mutually beneficial outcomes.

c) Assertive Communication

Assertive communication is stating your needs in a clear and respectful manner, yet being open to others' views. Example: Instead of saying, "You are wrong," say, "I see this differently. Let's discuss our perspectives."

d) The Power of Apology

Apologising is the most powerful weapon of conflict resolution, for it indicates admission of hurt, assumption of responsibility, and opens up avenues for reconciliation.

TURNING CHALLENGES INTO OPPORTUNITIES

While conflict can be challenging, it also provides opportunities for significant growth. Constructive handling strengthens the relationship, fosters the emergence of new thoughts, and enhances self-knowledge.

LEARNINGS FROM CONFLICT

- **Relationships:** Conflict establishes the foundation for building trust and understanding.
- **Creative Problem Solving:** The situations of conflict sharpen one's creativity and coordination.
- **Building Resilience:** Conflict resolution builds confidence and flexibility.

Conflict is an opportunity to grow and learn and form deeper connections with others and a chance to learn and grow and to be closer with others. Elements such as active listening, empathizing with people, and collaborative problem solving can turn challenges into opportunities for positive change.

Mastering the craft of conflict resolution, in everyday life, transforms discord into dialogue and opportunities into possibilities.

CHAPTER WRAP-UP

- **Conflict is Inevitable but Not Negative:** Conflict is a natural part of human interaction and can lead to growth and understanding if managed constructively.
- **Destructive vs. Constructive Conflict:** Destructive conflict leads to broken relationships, while constructive conflict can strengthen relationships and create solutions.
- **Focus on Interests, Not Positions:** Address the underlying needs and concerns rather than rigid demands.
- **Practice Active Listening:** Listen without interrupting, paraphrase to confirm understanding, and validate emotions.
- **Separate the Person from the Problem:** depersonalize the issue—now go about solving the problem.
- **Use Empathy and Respect:** Be responsive to their feelings and perspective—create an environment that allows constructive discussion.
- **Seek mutually beneficial solutions:** joint problem-solving that considers the mutual satisfaction of all parties' interests.
- **Build Conflict Resolution Competency:** Learn to deescalate, negotiate, engage in assertive communication, and use the power of apology.
- **Turn Conflict into Growth:** Take the conflict as an opportunity to strengthen relationships, enhance creativity, and build resilience.

84

CHAPTER EIGHT

PATIENCE: THE QUIET STRENGTH OF GROWTH

Patience is not the ability to wait, but the ability to keep a good attitude while waiting.

Patience is a virtue often overlooked but greatly needed in a world of instant gratification and constant noise. It is a silent strength, a skill that allows us to endure challenges, build resilience, and navigate the complexities of life with grace.

Patience is not passive; it is active, requiring intentional effort to pause, reflect, and persevere. Patience is the ability to handle difficult situations, delays, or setbacks without getting frustrated or upset. It's about staying calm, even when things don't go the way you hoped.

Patience covers more than just waiting—it's about attitude and method. Whether you're dealing with personal challenges, navigating tricky work situations, or interacting with others, patience is what keeps you steady and grounded.

WHY PATIENCE IS SO IMPORTANT?

Patience helps us think clearly, make better choices, and stay positive, even when things are tough. It allows us to manage our emotions, which leads to less stress and healthier relationships.

In both our personal and professional lives, patience can make the difference between a chaotic reaction and a thoughtful response.

It helps us to pause, reflect, and respond wisely rather than impulsively. It provides a sense of peace and calm that is crucial for making well-informed decisions.

Imagine trying to solve a problem when you are impatient. Your mind is restless, your body feels tense, and the solution seems impossible, right?

With patience, however, you can think more creatively, consider different perspectives, and ultimately make choices that are better for everyone involved.

IMPORTANCE OF PATIENCE IN SOCIAL WORK

In social work, patience is a must-have skill. Social workers often find themselves in challenging situations, needing to help people through their toughest moments. Patience is what lets them build trust, guide effectively, and work towards positive outcomes, even when progress seems slow.

Here are some reasons why patience matters in social work:

- **Establishing Trust with Clients:** Individuals frequently approach social workers with intricate, multifaceted problems that require time to resolve. Patience lets social workers listen, giving clients the space they need to open up and share their stories at their own pace. You cannot rush trust, and it takes time and effort to build a genuine connection.
- **Navigating Complex Cases:** The problems that social workers face are often complicated, involving issues like mental health, housing, project implementation, or family dynamics. We can't always resolve these challenges quickly.

Patience helps social workers stay committed, even when the process takes time. Understanding that change is a gradual process helps both the client and the social worker work collaboratively toward small, steady steps of progress.

- **Managing Emotional Stress:** Social work is emotionally demanding. Patience helps social workers keep their own stress levels in check, allowing them to remain calm and provide the best care for those they serve. This helps them manage client stress and their own emotions, preventing burnout and maintaining their health.

Patience is also essential for giving clients the support they need in moments of vulnerability. Many clients are hesitant to trust, and they may have experienced repeated disappointments in their lives.

A social worker who remains patient can help clients overcome these barriers, allowing them to feel heard, validated, and encouraged.

PATIENCE IN EVERYDAY LIFE

Patience isn't just for the workplace; it's a valuable quality in everyday life. Whether you're waiting in a long line, dealing with a difficult person, or working toward a long-term goal, patience keeps you from feeling frustrated and helps you keep a positive outlook.

Imagine trying to learn something new, like cooking or playing a musical instrument. If things don't go well right away, it's easy to become discouraged. Patiently focusing on the process rather than the result lets you enjoy the journey and reach your goal.

Another example is in relationships. When conflicts come up, patience lets you listen to the other person without reacting too quickly. This leads to better conversations and stronger, healthier connections. Patience plays a crucial role in fostering understanding and compassion in relationships.

In parenting, patience is especially important. Children learn and grow at their own pace, and as a parent, you often have to wait for your child to understand a lesson or develop a skill. Getting frustrated only makes things more difficult for both you and your child. By staying patient, you create a supportive environment where learning can happen naturally and joyfully.

HOW TO CULTIVATE PATIENCE IN REAL LIFE

Developing patience takes practice, but it's worth it. Here are some tips to help you grow your patience in your everyday life:

1. Practice Mindfulness

Do you often feel impatient or frustrated? Mindfulness can help you notice these feelings before they take over. When you feel impatience creeping in, pause, take a deep breath, and focus on the present moment. Mindfulness allows you to observe your emotions without reacting to them.

How to Achieve It:

Take a few minutes each day to practice mindfulness. This could be as simple as focusing on your breath, listening to the sounds around you, or just observing your thoughts.

Over time, this practice can help you react to challenges with more patience.

For example, if you're waiting for an important email response, rather than refreshing your inbox repeatedly, take that time to focus on your breathing or appreciate something around you.

2. Set Realistic Expectations

Are you expecting things to happen too quickly? Impatience often results from unrealistic expectations. Setting realistic goals and timelines can help you stay calm during the process.

Life rarely happens on our preferred schedule, and learning to accept this can lead to greater peace.

How to Achieve It:

Break big tasks into smaller steps, and celebrate each small win. For example, if you're working on a big project, focus on completing one section at a time instead of getting overwhelmed by the whole thing. Setting small, achievable goals will make it easier to stay motivated and patient.

3. Focus on What You Can Control

Impatience often arises when we try to control things beyond our reach. Recognize what you can change and let go of what you can't. Accepting the limits of your control is an important aspect of building patience.

How to Achieve It

Make a list of what you can and cannot control. When you start feeling frustrated, remind yourself to focus on the things within your control. This change in perspective can help reduce feelings of impatience.

For example, if you're waiting for a bus that's late, focus on how you can use that time, listen to music, or talk to a friend instead of worrying about when it will arrive.

4. Practice Deep Breathing

How do you respond when you're under stress? Taking a few deep breaths can help calm both your mind and body, letting you respond with patience instead of impulsiveness. It's a simple but effective way to reset when impatience starts building up.

How to Achieve It:

When impatience starts to build, take a pause and breathe deeply. Inhale through your nose, hold for a few seconds, then exhale slowly. This simple practice can help you regain your calm. Deep breathing activates your parasympathetic nervous system, which helps relax your body and mind.

5. Reframe the situation.

Do you see challenges as negative? Sometimes, impatience comes from seeing situations as problems. Rethinking them as growth opportunities may help you be patient.

How to Achieve It:

Instead of becoming frustrated while stuck in traffic, use that time to listen to a podcast or reflect on your blessings.

This change in perspective can turn a frustrating situation into something positive. Learning to reframe challenges can help you see the value in waiting and find meaning in the experience.

6. Avoid Instant Gratification

We've grown accustomed to instant gratification in our world. Learning to delay gratification can help you build patience. It teaches you to appreciate the process rather than just the outcome.

How to Achieve It:

Practice waiting for small things, like holding off on eating a treat or saving up for something you want instead of buying it right away. These small acts of self-control can help you grow your patience over time.

For instance, if you're tempted to buy a new gadget impulsively, remind yourself of a long-term financial goal you're working toward and how patience will help you achieve it.

7. Learn from Nature

The natural world's timeline can teach patience. Trees take years to grow, flowers bloom in their season, and animals follow natural rhythms. Nature moves slowly, yet it accomplishes everything.

How to Achieve It

Spend time outdoors and observe the natural world. Notice how things unfold in their own time. This can help you internalize the idea that good things take time and that waiting is beautiful.

8. Practice Self-Compassion

Often, we are impatient with ourselves. We want to be perfect, and when we fall short, we become frustrated. Practicing self-compassion means accepting that it's okay to make mistakes and understanding that growth is a gradual process.

How to Achieve It

When you catch yourself being overly critical or impatient with yourself, take a moment to treat yourself with kindness. Speak to yourself the way you would speak to a close friend who is struggling.

This will make you more patient and overall happier.

DON'TS OF PATIENCE

- **Don't Rush Yourself:** Don't put pressure on yourself to get things done quickly. Rushing can lead to mistakes and increased frustration. Take your time and do things thoughtfully.
- **Don't Compare Yourself to Others:** Everyone moves at their own pace. Comparing yourself to others can make you feel impatient and unhappy. Focus on your own journey. Everyone's circumstances are different, and progress is relative.
- **Don't Avoid Challenges:** Patience grows when you face challenges, not when you avoid them. Embrace difficult situations as chances to learn and build resilience. The more you practice patience, the stronger it becomes.
- **Don't Let Frustration Take Over:** When things don't go as planned, frustration can easily take over. Instead, take a deep breath and remember that setbacks are a normal part of life. Remind yourself that even successful people face delays and challenges.
- **Don't Expect Immediate Results:** Personal growth takes time. Don't expect immediate results from your efforts. Patience is about understanding that meaningful change happens gradually, not instantly.

Patience is a powerful tool for navigating both personal and professional challenges. In the field of social work, patience enables social workers to establish trust with their clients, provide support during challenging times, and navigate intricate situations with poise. In everyday life, patience helps us keep a positive attitude, nurture healthy relationships, and achieve our goals without feeling overwhelmed by stress.

Cultivating patience takes time, practice, and the courage to face challenges head-on. By practicing mindfulness, setting realistic expectations, focusing on what you can control, and viewing setbacks as opportunities, you can build patience and resilience. With patience, you'll be better prepared to handle setbacks, face obstacles, and lead a more balanced, fulfilling life.

Remember, patience is not about passively waiting; it's about actively enduring with grace.

WHAT STANDS OUT

- **Patience is an attitude:** It involves more than just waiting. It's about how you wait and the mindset you keep.
- **Practice Mindfulness:** Be aware of your emotions and respond to challenges with patience.
- **Set Realistic Expectations:** Avoid frustration by setting achievable goals and timelines.
- **Focus on What You Can Control:** Let go of what's out of your control and focus on what you can influence.
- **Take Deep Breaths:** Deep breathing can help you stay calm and patient.
- **Reframe Challenges:** See obstacles as opportunities for growth instead of as problems.
- **Avoid Instant Gratification:** Practice waiting to build patience and resilience.
- **Don't Compare Yourself to Others:** Stay focused on your own progress and journey.
- **Embrace Challenges:** Face challenges head-on to cultivate patience and grow stronger.
- **Practice self-compassion:** Treat yourself with kindness when things don't go as planned.
- **Learn from Nature:** Observe the natural world to understand the value of time and patience.

CHAPTER NINE

97

BEING NON-JUDGMENTAL

Empathy begins where judgement ends

Have you ever found yourself making quick judgments about someone based on their appearance or a single action? It's quite simple to do, and most of us have been guilty of it at some point. But what if we could practice seeing the world without immediately labelling or judging others? The principle of a non-judgmental attitude is to choose to observe without hastily drawing conclusions.

It's not about turning off our thoughts but instead being open to understanding without imposing our biases or preconceived notions.

This is more than just a skill; it's a fundamental principle of social work.

However, you might be wondering if this book is about social work skills, right?

The reason I've included this principle here is because it plays a vital role in shaping effective and compassionate practice. It's a way of being—a mindset that can lead to richer, more compassionate interactions with others.

Why is this so important? Because our world is changing. Every day, we meet people from different walks of life, each with their own stories, struggles, and dreams.

The ability to be non-judgmental helps us understand those stories without putting them in a box. For me, being non-judgmental means accepting people as they are, without trying to fit them into my expectations.

WHAT IS NON JUDGEMENTAL ATTITUDE?

In social work, a non-judgmental attitude is not just helpful, but it's essential. Vulnerable, mistake-making, or diverse people are often social workers' clients. To help effectively, social workers must approach every person with respect and without preconceived notions.

Imagine a social worker meeting someone struggling with addiction. If they judge this person based on stereotypes, they might dismiss their pain or overlook the underlying issues contributing to the addiction. Instead, approaching them with empathy and without judgment can lead to a better understanding of their needs and how to support them in making positive changes.

This principle is what allows social workers to truly connect with their clients. It builds trust and creates a safe environment where individuals feel heard and accepted. A person is more likely to open up, share honestly, and participate in the process of change when they perceive no judgment.

A non-judgmental attitude also helps social workers navigate ethical challenges. It prevents them from letting their personal biases interfere with their professional responsibilities.

Whether dealing with issues related to mental health, substance abuse, or family dynamics, maintaining a non-judgmental stance ensures that clients receive the support they need without feeling shamed or marginalized.

NON-JUDGMENTAL ATTITUDE IN EVERYDAY LIFE

You might be wondering, "How can being non-judgmental help me in my daily life?" Well, let's face it. Opinions inundate our world constantly. Social media, news channels, and even conversations with friends all invite us to pass judgment. But what if, just for a moment, you paused and chose not to judge? What if you decided to listen more and assume less?

Imagine this: You see someone lose their temper in public. Your first thought might be, "Wow, they have no self-control." But what if you reframed that thought? Perhaps they are enduring a particularly challenging period. Maybe they just received terrible news.

When you stop judging, you open yourself up to empathy. You might never know what's truly going on with that person, but choosing not to judge can make you more compassionate and less reactive.

In relationships, being non-judgmental can be a game-changer. When a friend or partner comes to you with a problem, do you immediately start thinking about what they did wrong or how they could have handled it better? It's effortless to succumb to such a mindset.

But instead, try just listening. Allow them to express themselves without any sense of analysis or criticism. It can deepen your relationships, build trust, and make others feel valued.

Even in self-reflection, being non-judgmental can make a big difference. How often do you criticize yourself for not being competent enough or for making mistakes? By practicing a non-judgmental attitude toward yourself, you can replace harsh self-criticism with understanding. It doesn't mean ignoring your flaws. It means acknowledging them without beating yourself up.

A non-judgmental attitude allows you to see yourself and others with kindness. Imagine you're trying to learn a new skill, like painting. It's straightforward to criticize yourself for not being proficient at it right away. But being non-judgmental means giving yourself the grace to be a beginner, to make mistakes, and to learn without feeling like you're failing. This creates a healthier mindset and encourages growth without fear.

CULTIVATING A NON-JUDGMENTAL ATTITUDE

Developing a non-judgmental attitude is not something that happens overnight. It takes practice and intentionality. Here are some ways you can cultivate this principle in your life:

1. Notice your judgments.

The first step to being non-judgmental is to become aware of when you are judging. It's natural to make quick judgments. We all do it. The key is to catch yourself when it happens.

How to Achieve It:

Throughout your day, pay attention to your thoughts. When you find yourself judging someone, take a step back and ask yourself why. What assumptions are you making? Simply acknowledging these judgments can help you begin to shift your mindset. Not stopping judgment, but being aware and choosing how to respond.

2. Ask questions instead of assumptions.

Instead of making assumptions, get curious. When you catch yourself forming an opinion about someone, try asking yourself questions like, "What might this person be going through?" or "Why might they have acted this way?" Curiosity is a powerful antidote to judgment.

How to Achieve It:

The next time someone cuts you off in traffic, instead of getting angry, ask yourself what might have caused them to rush. Maybe they're late for an important meeting or dealing with an emergency.

It doesn't mean excusing bad behaviour, but it does mean seeing people as more than their actions. By being curious, you allow yourself to understand the complexity of human behaviour.

3. Use "I" statements.

In work and everyday interactions, using "I" statements can help prevent judgment. Instead of saying, "You're wrong for doing that," try saying, "I feel concerned when this happens." It shifts the focus from placing blame to expressing your perspective, which is less likely to make the other person feel judged.

How to Achieve It:

Practice using "I" statements in difficult conversations.

For example, instead of saying, "You never listen to me," try, "I feel unheard when I don't get a chance to share my thoughts."

Although it's a subtle shift, it significantly impacts the reception of your message. Using "I" statements shows that you're willing to express your feelings without making the other person defensive.

4. Practice Mindfulness

Mindfulness is about staying present in the moment without judgment. It helps you observe your thoughts and emotions as they arise, without reacting to them. When you practice mindfulness, you create space between your thoughts and your reactions, making it easier to choose a non-judgmental response.

How to Achieve It:

Set aside a few minutes each day for mindfulness meditation. Sit quietly, focus on your breath, and notice any thoughts that come up. When you notice a judgmental thought, let it go and return your focus to your breathing.

Over time, this practice will help you become more aware of your judgments in everyday life. Mindfulness also helps you become more patient, which is an important aspect of non-judgmental behaviour.

5, Put Yourself in Others' Shoes

Empathy is a key part of being non-judgmental. When you try to see things from another person's perspective, it's harder to judge them. Everyone has a story, and everyone faces struggles that aren't always visible.

How to Achieve It:

The next time someone does something that bothers you, take a moment to imagine what their life might be like. What pressures might they be facing? How might their experiences have shaped their behaviour?

This exercise can help you replace judgment with understanding. Empathy isn't about excusing harmful behaviour but about understanding where it might come from and responding in a way that is constructive.

6. Challenge Stereotypes

We often judge based on stereotypes we've learned over time. Challenging these stereotypes is an important part of cultivating a non-judgmental attitude.

How to Achieve It:

Take note of any stereotypes you hold, whether about a particular group of people, profession, or lifestyle. Educate yourself, seek out stories and perspectives that challenge those stereotypes, and be open to changing your views.

For example, if you hold a stereotype about a certain profession, talk to someone who works in that field and learn about their experiences. Challenging stereotypes can help you see people as individuals rather than as part of a category.

Let us understand how cultivating such an attitude can help us.

Let's say you're at work and a colleague is consistently late. Your first instinct might be to think, "They're lazy and don't care about their job."

But if you take a non-judgmental approach, you might instead think, "I wonder if they're dealing with something difficult at home." Maybe they have a sick family member or are struggling with transportation issues. Rather than hastily drawing conclusions, it would be beneficial to offer assistance or simply show understanding.

Another example could be at a family gathering where someone makes a comment that seems rude. Try thinking they're insecure or anxious instead of trying to hurt you. By choosing not to judge their comment, you might be able to respond in a way that diffuses tension rather than escalating it.

In a classroom setting, teachers who practice non-judgmental attitudes can create a more supportive environment for students.

Imagine a student who frequently disrupts class. Instead of labelling them as a "troublemaker," a teacher might consider what factors outside of school could be affecting their behaviour. Are they dealing with challenges at home? Are they struggling with a learning disability? By approaching the student with empathy, the teacher can provide support that addresses the root cause of the behaviour.

Thus, being non-judgmental is more than just a social work principle. It's a way of being that can transform our interactions with others and ourselves. In a world that's constantly changing, where people come from all walks of life, choosing to be nonjudgmental allows us to connect more deeply and understand more fully.

It's not always easy, and it takes practice, but the rewards are immense.

When we approach others without judgment, we create a space where real communication and understanding can happen. We stop seeing people as "right" or "wrong" and start seeing them as human—complex, flawed, and deserving of compassion. And perhaps most importantly, when we stop judging ourselves, we allow ourselves to grow without the weight of constant criticism.

Non-judgment is about acknowledging that everyone, including ourselves, is doing the best they can with the tools and knowledge they have. It's about replacing criticism with curiosity and harshness with empathy.

When we cultivate this attitude, we become more open, understanding, and capable of making meaningful connections.

CRUCIAL CONCEPTS

- **Judgment is natural**, but awareness is crucial: It's natural to judge, but the first step to being non-judgmental is recognizing when it happens.
- **Be Curious, Not Critical:** Replace assumptions with questions. Get curious about why people act the way they do.
- **Use "I" Statements:** Communicate your feelings without placing blame. It helps others feel heard rather than judged.
- **Practice Mindfulness:** Mindfulness helps you observe your thoughts without reacting. It creates space for non-judgmental responses.
- **Put Yourself in Others' Shoes:** Try to see things from another person's perspective. Empathy is the key to understanding without judging.
- **Challenge Stereotypes:** Acknowledge and challenge the stereotypes you hold. Be open to learning and changing your views.
- **Non-Judgmental Attitude is a Choice:** Every day, you have the choice to judge or to understand. Choose understanding.
- **Judging Yourself Less Helps You Grow:** When you refrain from harshly judging yourself, you pave the way for genuine growth and self-compassion.

By practicing these principles, you can cultivate a non-judgmental attitude that will improve your relationships, enhance your work, and lead to a more compassionate and understanding way of living. Life becomes richer when we let go of judgment and embrace humanity in ourselves and others.

CHAPTER TEN

SELF-CARE AND WELLBEING

You cannot pour from an empty cup. Take care of yourself first.

How long has it been since you've done something for yourself to nourish your mind and body? Well, we get so caught up in daily life that we forget to look after that one person who matters most—YOU. Self-care and well-being involve keeping the balance right and nourishing your mental, emotional, and physical health. It's finding time for yourself, thus recharging, reflecting, and being the very best you can.

Self-care is not luxury or indulgence. It is the intentional act of preventing illness, reducing stress, and bringing joy. Well-being refers to a general state of being comfortable, healthy, and happy. The two go hand in hand: without self-care, your well-being can suffer, and without well-being, your ability to take care of yourself and others is compromised.

Why is that? This is because life is inherently exciting, sometimes stressful, and tiring.

For example, because of job-related, family-related, or personal factors, everybody needs to take at least a bit of his/her time to heal himself/herself.

Have you ever thought about how you could use your phone if it wasn't charged for quite a while? Just as the phone cannot survive without electricity, we also cannot strive without proper care for our health.

THE IMPORTANCE OF SELF-CARE IN SOCIAL WORK

Self-care is the most vital aspect of social work. Social workers encounter the daily pains, struggles, and challenges of others. They help people through some of the toughest times of their lives. Before helping others, they must first take care of themselves. You can't pour from an empty cup.

Imagine a social worker who works long hours without taking any breaks, who constantly worries about the well-being of their clients, and who never takes time to relax or unwind. Over time, this worker will become exhausted, stressed, and eventually burnt out.

Burnout doesn't just affect the worker; it affects the quality of care they provide to clients. It's challenging to be patient, empathetic, and understanding when you're overwhelmed and drained.

That's why every social worker should embrace the skill of self-care. It actually brings balance to emotions, preventing the possibility of burnout and ultimately enabling them to be present and effective at work. Simply engaging in well-being activities, such as taking a walk, practicing meditation, spending quality time with relatives, or simply resting, can make a significant difference.

Self-care is not selfish. It is necessary to sustain the energy and well-being required to do the things you love in a healthy and lasting way.

Maintaining professional boundaries also involves self-care. It is easy to fall in love with the social lives of your clients in your social work practice. Indeed, empathy plays a crucial role in any social work job, but it's important to distinguish between empathy and over-identification.

By practicing self-care, social workers can maintain their effectiveness in providing support without becoming overwhelmed by their clients' struggles.

SELF-CARE IN EVERYDAY LIFE: HOW IT CAN HELP

Social workers are not the only ones who practice self-care. Everybody encounters problems—big and small—and the art of self-care enables a person to cope gracefully with them. How does self-care improve lives?

For one, self-care reduces stress.

There are days when everything seems to be going wrong, our to-do lists seem endless and unachievable, or even the simplest things seem to go wrong. Taking care of ourselves again, whether it be through reading books, bathing, or any other activity that helps us manage our stress levels, puts us right back on track.

Stress, if left unchecked, can have very serious effects on our mental and physical health, leading to anxiety, depression, and in more severe cases, physical illness. Self-care, therefore, is like a safety valve; it lets us release the tension before it becomes too much.

Self-care also brings a positive effect on our relationship because when one feels satisfied about himself/herself, he/she becomes more patient, understanding, and supportive toward people around them.

You know it's difficult to comfort a friend when you're exhausted, right? Taking care of your own needs enables you to be there for others. We can actually give our loved ones the attention and care they deserve when we are well-rested and emotionally balanced. We become better listeners, better partners, and better friends.

Self-care also helps our mental and emotional health.

All the activities that bring us joy, such as engaging in hobbies, spending time in nature, or simply spending time with friends, trigger the release of feel-good hormones that enhance our mood and overall well-being. Finding what works for you and prioritizing it in your life is crucial. When we put our happiness first, we lay the groundwork for resilience. Challenges in life are much easier to deal with when we have already built that emotional strength through self-care.

GROWING AN ART OF SELF-CARE AND WELLBEING

So, how can you cultivate self-care and well-being in daily life? Here are a few practical tips that can get you started:

1. Identify Your Needs

What recharges you? What makes you happy? Knowing what you need is step one in building self-care. People are different, so what works for someone else may not work for you. Maybe you recharge with alone time, or maybe it's friends time.

Take some time to reflect on what makes you happy. Write down what energizes you and what de-energizes you. Use that list to give priority to what enhances your well-being. Consider keeping a self-care journal, an activity where you can record things that make you feel positive and changes in your mood afterwards.

2. Set Boundaries

Have you become someone who finds it difficult to say no? The truth is, most people struggle with setting boundaries, despite it being a crucial aspect of self-care. You risk overcommitting and spreading too thin without boundaries. Practice doing it in small ways.

For example, if someone invites you to do something you don't have time for, do it politely. Remember that NO to others is actually YES to one's self.

Establishing healthy boundaries to safeguard your time and energy for your well-being teaches others to respect your limits. The truth is, it's not about erecting walls, but rather, it's about creating gates that allow in what is nourishing and keep out what is draining.

3. Make time for self-care.

Self-care doesn't happen by accident. One must intentionally engage in self-care. It's simple to say, "I'll do it when I have time," but in life, that's usually a lie. To make self-care a priority, schedule it. Schedule time each day or every week for self-care activities.

Write it into your calendar just like you would any other appointment. Whether it is 30 minutes of yoga, a walk in the park, or just sitting quietly with a cup of tea, make it non-negotiable. This is treating your self-care time as sacred; that's an investment in well-being that pays off in thousands of ways.

4. Learn to be mindful

Mindfulness is being present in the moment. It connects you to how you feel and what you need. This way, mindfulness can help you recognize when you are getting overwhelmed and act on that feeling to take care of yourself. Try mindfulness meditation for a few minutes a day. Sit quietly and focus on your breath. Be aware of your thoughts without judgment.

Mindfulness can also be as easy as paying attention to your senses—what you can see, hear, feel, taste, and smell—at any particular moment. Mindfulness, apart from easing stress, increases our appreciation for little joys in life that we hardly pay attention to.

5. Prioritize Sleep

How productive is your sleep at night? Actually, perhaps the most important aspect of self-care is sleep. Poor sleep affects our mood, energy, and much more.

Start a bedtime routine so you're winding down. Try to stay off screens and regulate the sleeping area at bedtime.

Most importantly, try to get into bed around the same time every night. More sleep will greatly benefit your mental as well as physical health. A good night's sleep has everyone in a great mood in the morning.

6. Engage in physical activity.

A beneficial and healthy way to take care of the body and mind is through exercising. Exercise releases endorphins, natural mood boosters. It also helps reduce one's stress and improves the quality of sleep. Find something you like—exercise, be it dancing, jogging, yoga, or playing a sport.

Finding an activity you enjoy rather than forcing yourself to exercise. Even short walks do a lot for well-being. Joining a class or finding a workout partner can also serve as a form of social engagement, combining two forms of self-care into one.

7. Connect with others.

Every person requires contact with others as part of optimal health. For this reason, some individuals may find emotional support and a sense of belonging by spending time with loved ones, engaging in conversations with friends, or participating in community groups. Actively call, meet up with, or text friends or family regularly.

Even making a quick phone call or having a coffee can make huge differences. Join a club or group that interests you, as it may help you make new friends. Then, you will meet other people and make more friends.

Asking for help when you need it is another way to take good care of yourself. No walking alone in life. A person who is surrounded by connections, bonds, and relationships maintains good emotional health.

8. Do something you love.

What do you like to do? Whether it's painting, gardening, cooking, playing a musical instrument, or whatever you enjoy doing, doing it is a wonderful way to nurture yourself. It's like self-expression, relaxation, and enjoyment. Plan for hobbies—even if it's only minutes a day.

Activities you enjoy might improve your mood, reduce stress, and increase your sense of well-being. Start with small doses of joy. These small doses may act as a buffer against stress and can improve emotional balance.

9. Practice Gratitude

Gratitude is an incredibly powerful tool for building well-being. If we focus on what goes right in life, we displace lack with what is present. To do so, write down three things for which you are grateful every day, no matter how big or small they may be—a beautiful sunset, a friendly friend, or a well-prepared meal.

Practicing gratitude improves your mood so you can increase the levels of happiness and remember that you're still privileged on any given day, however bad it gets.

THE DON'TS OF SELF-CARE

- **Don't Feel Guilty for Taking Time for Yourself:** Self-care is not selfish; it's necessary. Taking time for yourself doesn't mean you're neglecting others. In fact, by caring for yourself, you're better able to care for those around you.
- **Do not say yes to everything:** it's lovely to say yes to everybody, but it's very easy to become overcommitted; know your limits, and do not be afraid to say no when you need to protect your energy.
- **Admit Your Needs:** Recognize when you're feeling overworked, tired, or stressed. If you fail to monitor these signs, you may face significant problems in the future. Please listen to your body and mind and act when necessary.
- **Don't compare yourself with others:** self-care is different for every individual. As with everything else, what works for one won't work for you. Find what works for you and stick to it; do not worry about what others are doing.
- **Take care of yourself before you burn out:** Self-care is proactive, not reactive. Take care of yourself before you become exhausted. Integrate this into your lifestyle to prevent burnout from occurring.

Self-care and well-being are not something luxurious; they are the very foundations of living a balanced and fulfilling life. Either you are a social worker under immense pressure, or you are simply seeking an effective way to enhance your daily life. Caring for yourself is the base from which everything else springs into life. It involves being intentional, setting boundaries, and making time for activities that nourish your mind, body, and soul.

Giving self-care a priority will improve your quality of life and make you a better friend, partner, worker, and human being. It will give you energy, patience, and resilience for whatever lies ahead.

Remember, self-care is not selfish. It's the most loving thing you can do for yourself and those around you.

LESSONS LEARNED

- **Self-Care is not Selfish:** Taking care of yourself is crucial for your well-being and in being present for others.
- **What Works for You:** Self-care is highly individual. Identify things that energize and are fun.
- **Set Boundaries:** Learn How to Say No and Protect Time and Energy.
- **Make self-care a top priority:** Treat time scheduled for yourself as any other important appointment.
- **Practice mindfulness:** Being present and attuned to thoughts and feelings without judgment.
- **Get enough sleep:** Develop good sleep hygiene for excellent health and well-being.
- **Move Your Body:** Physical activity is a good mood elevator and also reduces stress.
- **Connect with others:** Mankind needs relationships to have good emotional well-being.
- **Do what you love:** Use spare time for hobbies and other interests that bring you pleasure.
- **Focus on Your Body:** Learn to listen to and react to your stress signals or even signs of exhaustion.
- **Practice gratitude:** Stay focused on the good in life, and that will in itself enhance your welfare.
- **Self-Care Proactivity:** Establish self-care as a routine instead of waiting until you're exhausted.

Self-care is embracing yourself; this means that you lead a healthier, happier life and thus a more balanced, joyful life. Remember, you deserve positive feelings, and self-treatment is the first step to a happier, healthier you.

CHAPTER ELEVEN

FROM LEARNING TO LEADING

You can do anything. You just have to be determined

Throughout this book, we had the opportunity to test these skills, which are highly relevant to the practice of social workers and equally useful in solving problems in daily life. We had a great time learning about the skills, principles, histories, and importance of empathy, communication, organization, etc. in social work.

We discussed empathy as access to true understanding and relating, active listening as the core of a good conversation, and critical thinking to make better choices. We had topics that had to do with conflict resolution, patience, and not judging. And lastly, we talked about self-care and well-being.

These are skills that go beyond social workers; they are tools that everyone can use to make both our professional and personal lives more accessible, not just to live without pain but to live a better life.

In this chapter, we will delve into how all the previously discussed skills can integrate seamlessly into our daily routines, interactions, and other relationships, thereby fostering stronger bonds, improving our judgment, and enhancing our quality of life.

KEY TAKEAWAYS FROM PREVIOUS CHAPTERS

- Let's recall some key takeaway points before we actually go ahead and apply these skills:
- Empathy is about walking in someone's shoes and therefore understanding them and creating trust in building genuine relationships.

- Body language, tone, and listening are all parts of the interactive process of communication.
- Active listening involves all your attention to the speaker, understanding the speaker's message, and responding thoughtfully. This is the way to a deeper relationship.
- Organizational skills bring order out of chaos. They help us manage our time, set priorities, and allow us to meet our purposes.
- Critical thinking enables an objective look at the situation and then fetches information to make the decision.
- In this sense, conflict resolution involves transforming challenges into opportunities. It involves deliberating on disputes with empathy and making progress in problem-solving.
- Patience is the ability to remain calm and composed in the face of setbacks. It helps people tackle such a situation without losing their cool and making grave mistakes.
- Non-judgmental attitude is the principle that allows knowing other people without imposing our biases on them. It Favors acceptance and welcome.
- Self-care and well-being form essential components in maintaining balance that prevents burnout.
- Taking care of oneself is crucial for being more present with others.

All of these skills tie into each other in an amazing way. They lay the groundwork for having a healthy relationship, problem-solving skills, and personal growth.

Let's see how we can put these skills into play in our lives now.

APPLY SOCIAL WORK SKILLS IN YOUR LIFE

Social work skills are not something we keep to the workplace alone. They can revolutionize how we relate to the world around us. Here are some concrete ways we can begin to apply them to everyday life:

a) Empathy in real life.

Empathy is the foundation of excellent, genuine relationships. Every day, we interact with numerous individuals who are facing various difficulties, whether it's a co-worker you can't stand, a friend who can bring you down, or a family member who is struggling with a particular issue. Instead of hastily drawing conclusions or prescribing solutions, consider placing yourself in their position. Question yourself how you would feel if you were in his shoes.

For instance, perhaps a colleague has been short-tempered lately. Don't consider that they are being rude; perhaps they are dealing with something difficult. Approach them with empathy. Perhaps you could inquire about their well-being or simply offer a listening ear. Empathy can transform a potentially negative situation into a positive moment of connection.

b) Communicating The Art of Expression and Listening

Good communication is not just talking; it's expression and listening. Practice being fully present in everyday conversations by taking away all distractions, maintaining eye contact, and showing an interest in what the other person has to say.

For instance, when sitting down with the family to have dinner, do not immediately go for your phone but instead engage meaningfully as you share a meal.

Say "What has been the best part of your day so far?" "Is there something on your mind?"

c) Active Listening: The Heart of Connection

Active listening is a crucial skill that can significantly transform your relationship. Active listening involves not only hearing the other person's words but also their emotions and intentions. So, start practicing listening without formulating an approach in your daily life. Listen to the speaker fully and acknowledge their feelings.

For instance, if a friend has a problem that he brings to you, do not jump in to fix it for him. Listen to his problem, nod at appropriate places, and say something like, "That really sounds tough. I'm here for you." At times, people seek comfort in active listening.

d) Organization in a busy world

Organization is not only about keeping your workspace clean; it also includes managing how you use your time, prioritizing things, and reducing your stress levels. In daily life, organization helps a person feel much more in control and less overwhelmed.

Start your day by jotting down what you plan to do. Put checks on those that you deem most significant for the day and address them one after the other.

This simple habit helps you stay organized and prevents you from becoming confused when remembering what you need to do. Organization is crucial for maintaining balance in this hectic world.

e) Use critical thinking to make better decisions.

Basically, critical thinking is weighing information and making decisions based on evidence rather than emotion. Being a useful tool in solving problems about decision-making in life also helps prevent impulsive choices.

For instance, you may desire a new gadget. However, do not act on a whim; take your time thinking through the decision. Do you need it? Can you afford it at this moment? Are there other alternatives?

You can only make decisions that are in line with your long-term goals after objectively weighing the situation.

f) Solving conflict with empathy and understanding

Conflicts are inevitable in life, but the difference lies in how to tackle them. Avoiding or becoming defensive is not the appropriate approach. Tackle it with empathy and a spirit of resolving the issue.

Example: If you disagree with your friend, instead of blaming him or getting angry, try to see things from his point of view. Employ "I" statements, such as "I felt hurt when you said that because I care about our friendship." This reduces defensiveness and allows a positive conversation to occur.

g) Patience Applied in Testing Times

Dealing with unpleasant situations without becoming overwhelmed by them requires patience. In everyday life, there are innumerable moments that confront our patience, like waiting in a long line, dealing with a problematic person, or facing setbacks at work.

Consider the scenario where you find yourself waiting on yourself due to a late schedule and traffic congestion. Breathe deeply, reminding yourself that there are things beyond your control. You can use this time to listen to the soft music or even to a podcast that interests you. Patience serves as a calming force and helps you avoid getting overwhelmed with stressful feelings.

h) Being Non-Judgmental: Look Beyond the Facade

Being non-judgmental simply means approaching people without a preconceived notion about them. It helps us see people as they are, not as we want them.

Example: Imagine that you come across a person whose lifestyle or belief system is different. Instead of judging him or her by your own experiences, you approach with curiosity and openness. You ask them questions to learn more about their perspective. This attitude fosters understanding and breaks barriers.

(i) Prioritizing self-care and well-being

Self-care is spending quality time with oneself so as to become the best for others. The same principle applies in daily life: set aside time to engage in activities that bring you happiness, rest, or relaxation.

Example: Schedule time in your busy day for something that you enjoy: a book, exercise, or time out in the open. Make it non-negotiable. Taking care of yourself gives you more energy and positivity to share.

j) Ingrain gratitude into everyday life

It is that simple and powerful practice that changes your way of looking at life. It shifts your focus from what is lacking to what you have, fostering a positive outlook that permeates every aspect of your day.

Example: Start or end your day by writing down three things you're grateful for. They can be as simple as the morning sunshine, a kind word from a friend, or a delicious meal. Gratitude helps us stay grounded and appreciative, even when times are tough.

An action plan for applying these skills

Those social work skills do not have to make daily life chaotic. Here's a plan of action for integrating them into daily routines:

1. Begin small: Learn one skill a week. To demonstrate this, engage in active listening during your conversations for the entire week, observing the impact on your relationships and the reactions of others when they truly feel heard.

2. Reflect on Your Day: Take a little time in the evening to think of how you have interacted with people. Did you show empathy? How often do you judge someone without understanding their story? This will make you aware and influence positive changes.

3. Set Intentions: Each day starts out with determining what your intention is for that day. It might be, "Today I will listen without interrupting," or "Today I will be patient in difficult situations." That keeps you focused on your intentions.

4. Practice Self-Compassion: Remember, change is a slow process. OK, you won't always get it right. Let your self-compassion guide you. Provide yourself with kindness, acceptance, and nonjudgment as you build these skills.

5. Seek feedback: Ask trusted friends or family members for feedback. You could ask, "Do you notice any differences in how I listen or communicate?" Such constructive criticism can help you notice areas for improvement and celebrate your progress.

6. Celebrate your small wins. Each time you successfully apply the skill, take a moment to celebrate it. Whether you were resolving conflict peacefully or holding your patience in a tight moment, take a moment to recognize your efforts and progress.

7. Write it down: Keep a diary and write about your progress. Writing things down not only helps reflect but also allows you to see how much distance you have covered over time.

8. Create a Support System: Develop relationships that promote positive thinking. One may come along on a journey with friends or family members who can inspire you, remind you of your goal, and cherish all your successes with you.

9. Apply Them at Work: At the office or working from home, apply these skills to improve the work environment. Listen actively at the meeting, empathize when interacting with colleagues, and keep yourself organized to meet deadlines efficiently.

10. Use Reminders: Place sticky reminders around your home or workplace: "Be Patient," "Listen Actively," "Practice Empathy," and so on. Visual reminders can be effective at keeping these skills at the forefront of your mind.

Empathy, communication, listening, organization, critical thinking, conflict resolution, patience, being non-judgmental, and self-care are all tools of a social worker, but they are also life skills that may change how one lives and interacts in this world.

When applied in daily life, it empowers individuals to make more informed and superior choices, and to confront challenges with resilience and elegance.

Change doesn't happen overnight; inch by slow inch, we steadily make small actions that turn into habits within us.

Imagine living in close relationships with people, peacefully resolving issues, and giving yourself what you need without feeling guilty.

This life is possible—and it starts with making what you learn here a lived reality.

Life is constantly learning, and every step you make could be perceived as a new lesson. Apply these skills to your life and watch your relationships, stress, and well-being improve.

It is up to you to be that force of change for yourself and all the people around you.

A BLESSING FOR GROWTH AND SUCCESS

As we close this journey of skills that may make our lives more fulfilling, let us pray for those who embark on this path of self-improvement and growth.

बुद्धिहीन तनु जानिके, सुमिरौं पवन-कुमार।
बल बुधि बिद्या देहु मोहिं, हरहु कलेस बिकार।।

Budhiheen Tanu Jaanike, Sumirau Pavan Kumar
Bal Buddhi vidya dehu Mohi, Harahu kalesh vicar

- Hanuman Chalisa

Translation: "Knowing myself to be ignorant, I remember you, O Hanuman, son of the Wind. Give me strength, wisdom, and knowledge, and take away all my misery and imperfections.

May Lord Hanuman bless all readers of this book with the strength to apply these skills. May the reader of this book learn wisdom in handling life's challenges with compassion for uplifting oneself and others. May your journey be filled with growth, peace, and success. Jai Hanuman!

FINAL THOUGHTS

- **Empathy**: Show empathy for others by putting yourself in their position.
- **Communication**: Engage in meaningful communication by speaking clearly and listening.
- **Active listening**: give full focus to the speaker and respond with understanding appropriately.
- **Organization**: Manage time and tasks to reduce stress and maintain balance.
- **Critical thinking**: distinguish between reality and fiction and give wise decisions.
- **Conflict Resolution**: Dispose of disputes with empathy and a solution-focused approach.
- **Patience**: Be calm when faced with problems; that time will take care of everything.
- **Non-judgmental attitude**: treat people without prejudice and try to understand instead of judging.
- **Self-care**: Find time for things that help the body, soul, and mind.
- **Gratitude**: Practice gratitude to shift your focus toward the positive aspects of your life.

Keeping these skills always at the forefront of our minds and actively practicing them would make life and the lives of people around us better.

Remember, one cannot become the best without being consistent; every step brought people closer to a kinder, more connected, and fulfilling life.

A Note Of Thanks

Dear Readers, thank you for taking the time to read this book. Your curiosity, engagement, and willingness to explore these ideas mean the world to me. I hope the insights shared within these pages have inspired, challenged, and empowered you to bring positive change to your own life and the world around you.

Your support in reading this work is deeply appreciated, and I am truly grateful for your time and interest.

With sincere thanks,
Angel Protim Dutta

Bibliography

1. Barker, R. L. (2003). The Social Work Dictionary. 5th ed. Washington, DC: NASW Press.
2. Bhattacharya, S. (2003). Social work: An Integrated Approach. Deep and Deep Publications.
3. Brookfield, S. D. (2012). Teaching for Critical Thinking: Tools and Techniques to Help Students Question Their Assumptions. Jossey-Bass.
4. Brown, B. (2012). Daring greatly: How the courage to be vulnerable transforms the way we live, love, parent, and lead. Gotham Books.
5. Deutsch, M. (1973). The resolution of conflict: Constructive and destructive processes. Yale University Press.
6. Facione, P. A. (2015) Critical Thinking: What It Is and Why It Counts. Insight Assessment.
7. Fisher, R., Ury, W., & Patton, B. (2011). Getting to yes: Negotiating agreement without giving in. Penguin Books.
8. Friedlander, W. A. (1951). Introduction to Social Welfare. Prentice-Hall.
9. Gates, M. (2020). The moment of lift: How empowering women changes the world. Flatiron Books.
10. Gibbs, G. (1988). Learning by Doing: A Guide to Teaching and Learning Methods. Oxford Brookes University.
11. Gita Press. (1997). Shri Hanuman Chalisa. Gita Press.
12. Glaser, E. M. (1941). An Experiment in the Development of Critical Thinking. Teachers College, Columbia University.

13. Goleman, D. (1995). Emotional intelligence: Why it can matter more than IQ. Bantam Books.

14. Kabat-Zinn, J. (1990). Full catastrophe living: Using the wisdom of your body and mind to face stress, pain, and illness. Delta.

15. Kahneman, D. (2011). Thinking, Fast and Slow. Farrar, Straus and Giroux.

16. Keen, S. (2006). A theory of narrative empathy. Narrative, 14(3), 207–236. https://doi.org/10.1353/nar.2006.0015

17. Kendall, F. E. (2006). Understanding white privilege: Creating pathways to authentic relationships across race. Routledge.

18. Krznaric, R. & Blackbird. (2007). EMPATHY and the art of living.

19. Levine, P. A. (1997). Waking the tiger: Healing trauma. North Atlantic Books.

20. Lipman, M. (2003). Thinking in Education. Cambridge University Press.

21. Lorde, A. (1988). A burst of light: Essays. Firebrand Books.

22. Maslach, C., & Leiter, M. P. (2016). Burnout: A psychological perspective. Routledge.

23. Mead, M. (2005). Coming of age in Samoa. Harper Perennial Modern Classics.

24. National Association of Social Workers. (2021). Code of ethics. NASW Press.

25. Nayak, D., C.D.O.E. Education For All, & Utkal University. (2023). Master Of Social Work. In Utkal University, C.D.O.E. https://ddceutkal.ac.in/Syllabus/MSW/PAPER-1.pdf

26. Nichols, M. P. (2009). The lost art of listening: How learning to listen can improve relationships. Guilford

Press.

27. Paul, R., & Elder, L. (2006). The Thinker's Guide to Intellectual Standards. Foundation for Critical Thinking.

28. Paul, R., & Elder, L. (2014). Critical Thinking: Tools for Taking Charge of Your Professional and Personal Life. Pearson.

29. Payne, M. (2014). Modern social work theory. Oxford University Press.

30. Rheingold, H. (2002). Smart mobs: The next social revolution. Basic Books.

31. Rogers, C. R. (1980). A way of being. Houghton Mifflin Harcourt.

32. Rogers, C., & Farson, R. E. (1987). ACTIVE LISTENING. In R.G. Newman, M.A. Danzinger, M. Cohen (Ed.), Communicating in Business Today. D.C. Heath & Company. https://wholebeinginstitute.com/wp-content/uploads/Rogers_Farson_Active-Listening.pdf

33. Shirky, C. (2008). Here comes everybody: The power of organizing without organizations. Penguin Books.

34. Siegel, D. J. (2010). The mindful therapist: A clinician's guide to mindsight and neural integration. W. W. Norton & Company.

35. Talbot, D. (2024, February 6). Listening statistics. https://wordsrated.com/listening-statistics/

36. Tata Institute of Social Sciences (TISS). (n.d.). History and Vision. Retrieved from https://www.tiss.edu

37. Thompson, N. (2015). Understanding social work: Preparing for practice. Red Globe Press.

38. Tutu, D. (1999). No future without forgiveness. Image.

Notes & Reflections

144